A CONCISE HISTORY OF FRANCE

A CONCISE HISTORY OF

FRANCE

DOUGLAS JOHNSON

with 213 illustrations

THAMES AND HUDSON · LONDON

Frontispiece: The siege of La Rochelle,
the last Huguenot stronghold, in 1628

© 1971 *Thames and Hudson Ltd, London*

*Printed in Great Britain by
Jarrold and Sons Limited, Norwich*

ISBN 0 500 45008 0

Contents

Preface

A colleague once told me that when he wanted to find out about a subject he didn't read a book about it, he wrote a book about it. I have followed at least part of his advice; a wish to study the history of France from the earliest times has led to the writing of this book.

I must firstly express my gratitude to my wife. She has helped me in many ways and in particular she has removed much of the clumsiness of my style. I have benefited from the advice and encouragement of many friends and I would particularly like to thank Dr R. R. Davies, Prof. Harvey Mitchell, Mr J. A. North, Dr Pamela Pilbeam and Dr Nicola Sutherland. They are not, of course, responsible for my mistakes.

I would also like to thank Mr Stephen England and Miss Erica Gentle, of Thames and Hudson, for all their efforts on my behalf, and Mrs Katie Edwards for her skilful typing.

Douglas Johnson

Hampstead, London; Saint Servan-sur-mer

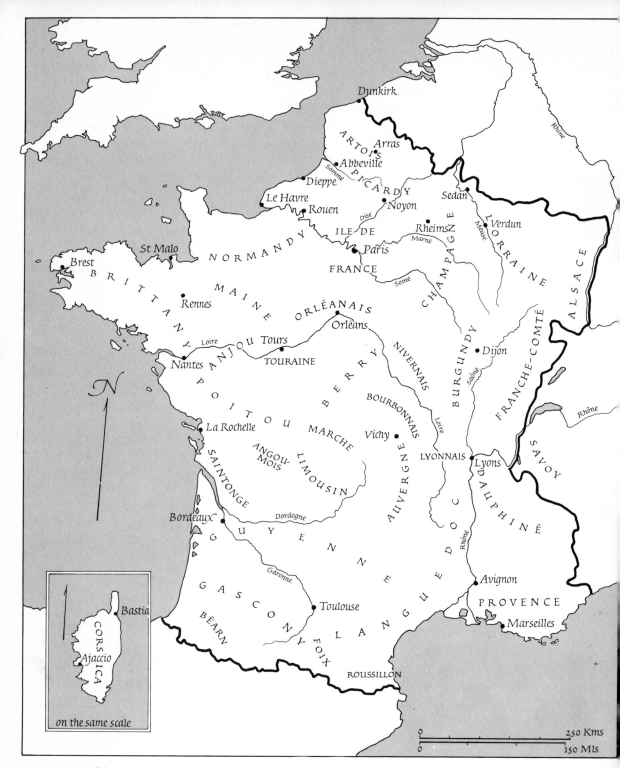

France of the Ancien Régime.

It is difficult to say when French history begins. For some it is Gaul which marks the beginning of France, and the Celts, particularly under Vercingetorix, have been seen as the original French nation. Others point out that the foundation of Marseilles about 600 B C, by Greeks from Ionia, is the first really accurate date of French history. In a similar way it has been argued that it is only with the Roman conquest that there can be any documented certainty about the French past, just as it is only then that there is any real sense of French unity. But for a long time these periods were thought so unimportant that historians began their accounts of France with the Frankish invasions. The baptism of Clovis, traditionally thought to have been in 496; the Treaty of Verdun in 843 which separated France from Germany and Lotharingia and created the historical entity of France; the year 987 which saw the first of the Capetians: these are moments which have also been seen as the effective beginnings of France.

In the nineteenth century, as the study of history became more self-assured, the great historians of France were agreed upon the nature of these beginnings. They stressed the diversity of French origins. For Guizot (1787–1874), as for

One of the earliest coins from the Greek colony of Massilia, the modern Marseilles (obverse and reverse).

Sismonde de Sismondi (1773–1842), there were the dual civilizations of Gaul and of Rome; for Michelet (1798–1874) there was in the beginning the character of the Celts of Gaul, 'the most sympathetic and the most perfectible of the human race', in contact with other peoples, Iberians, Greeks, Phoenicians, other Celts, and eventually, the Romans; Henri Martin (1810–83) spoke of the French as having the blood of all the other peoples of humanity mixed with their Gallic blood, and drew a picture of the French as Gauls by birth and character, Romans by their intelligence; Victor Duruy (1811–94) began with the Celts, the Iberians and the Belgae. And this diversity was not an inconsequential fact. Was it not this that explained the rich destiny of France? Guizot, delivering a famous set of lectures on French civilization in the 1820's, said that he would have chosen the civilization of some other European country had there been one which could have been equally great and instructive. It was in France that civilization appeared most complete and communicative, where it had most struck the imagination of Europe. Victor Duruy thought that French civilization was the résumé of modern civilization; the role that had been played by Athens and then by Rome had, in modern times, been assumed by France. And this attitude has persisted. Just as Seignobos, writing in 1933, looked to the diversity of French origins to explain what he called 'the international character of the French mind and the universal character of French literature', so other historians have looked back to tenacious elements in the French past which can explain the successive and different civilizations which have flowered in France.

This emphasis on diversity was not only historical; it was also geographical. It was suggested that France became France because Nature wished it so. The Greek geographer Strabo described the ease of communication which the great navigable rivers bestowed upon the country and saw in this a harmony deliberately created by a beneficent Providence. The nature of the soil, the deep penetration of maritime influences and the temperate climate, were the conditions which attracted a numerous population. But other geographers have emphasized the innumerable differences of soil, altitude and climate, so that the inhabitants of France have always lived lives which are different one from another. Just as there was never a French race, so there was never a French type. And it was a factor of geography that France, lying between the Mediterranean, the Atlantic and the English Channel, was a natural meeting-place for the routes of Western Europe. Whether taken as a whole or in her parts, France has to be seen in relation to her neighbours; more than most countries,

France has been susceptible to the currents, contacts and contingencies of other lands.

Nowadays it is natural to begin with the prehistoric age, since we are beginning to appreciate the extent and the interest of this enormous period in time. And it so happens that the signs of prehistoric habitation are more abundant in France than in many other countries. But it does not make these beginnings any the less mysterious. The earliest skulls found in France, like the Montmaurin mandible found in a cave in the lower Pyrenees, and the fragments of two skulls found at Fontéchevade, east of Angoulême, suggest that there might have been a 'homo sapiens' before Neanderthal man. The valley of the river Somme has yielded much information about the hand-axe culture of the Lower Palaeolithic period; we refer to these cultures as Abbevillian, which developed into Acheulian (Abbeville and Saint-Acheul being the eponymous towns near to Amiens), or as Chellean, after Chelles near to Paris where the chipped stone artifacts were first found. The discoveries of skeletons at Le Moustier, at La Chapelle-aux-Saints and at La Ferrassie, all in the Dordogne, show examples of Neanderthal men who both buried their dead and honoured them with ceremonial (stone-lined graves, special arrangements of stones and flints).

But the first clearly recognizable example of an advanced type of man ('the Apollo of prehistoric man' as he has been called, because he seemed more human than the allegedly brute-like Neanderthals) was Cro-Magnon man. It was in 1868 that workmen in Périgord unearthed a number of skeletons in a rock-shelter called Cro-Magnon near to Les Eyzies-de-Tayac. It was estimated that these men had lived about 20,000 to 30,000 years ago. Similar finds were made at Aurignac in the lower Pyrenees, and a skull found at Combe Capelle, in Périgord, ante-dates Cro-Magnon. But it is Cro-Magnon which has remained the most famous because it is in this region, the valley of the river Vézère in Dordogne, that these early settlers cease to be entirely shadowy figures known only by their tools and implements. We actually have a sense of a culture, because it is here, at La Madeleine, La Mouthe, Font de Gaume, Les Combarelles, Lascaux and at other places of which Les Eyzies is the centre, that there exist the famous cave drawings and paintings. The painted caves at Angoulême, Cahors and the Pyrenees are reasonably near by.

Cro-Magnon Man

It seems clear that these men continued to live the lives of hunters and food-gatherers. Agriculture was unknown and caves or rock-shelters were the normal dwelling-places. But they lived in a society which was relatively advanced.

11

Engraved pebble,
showing a reindeer.

The grave at Cro-Magnon contained evidence of trading contact with the sea, which was more than a hundred miles away. These men perfected their implements, using flint, bone, ivory and antler. They had a great many group activities. And parts of their caves, or specially chosen shelters, were decorated in such a way as to suggest that they were turned into sanctuaries. They drew or painted the animals which they hunted, such as reindeer, bison, mammoth, horses and stags; at Lascaux there are the great polychrome friezes of bulls and cows; at Font-de-Gaume there are rhinoceroses; at Cap Blanc there are carvings of horses, bison and an ox, at Anglès-sur-l'Anglin, in the Vienne department, there are carvings of women and animals, whilst in the rock-shelter at Laussel there are bas-reliefs. Often the animals are represented with realism, but the human figures are usually more crudely depicted, sometimes shown as part-animal, often with animal heads or marks. It is difficult not to believe that this art has a magico-religious significance; it must have been linked to some ritual operation designed for a community of hunters; it might be that the representation of an animal was thought to confer power upon those who lived in the cave. Certainly, this artist's view of the world, filled with a great variety of sexual symbols, shows a primitive society's preoccupation with life.

The caves and rock-shelters of Palaeolithic man are often decorated with paintings and carvings of the animals they hunted. *Above:* the great polychrome frieze of horses and deer in the cave of Lascaux. *Right:* a horse carved in high relief at Cap Blanc.

It is not easy to date these paintings closely. It seems that the period of cave-dwellers and cave-artists spreads over many thousands of years, and includes many different cultures for which no acceptable time-chart exists. Some caves, like Pech-Merle, near Cahors, have decorations which have been made over a very long period. At all events, these cultures must have come to an end with the slow melting of the glacial ice. The Palaeolithic, or Old Stone Age, is sometimes thought to have ended between about 10,000 and 8000 B C, followed by the Neolithic, or New Stone Age. Between them occurred the so-called Mesolithic period, represented in France by the cave of the Mas d'Azil in the Ariège, which is a sort of restrained version of the preceding culture. In the Neolithic age men learned to polish stone tools, to live by agriculture, to dwell in houses and villages, make pottery and weave cloth. Populations grew and men used the wheel and had various sorts of water-craft. They eventually forged and cast metals. So great a series of changes has been called the Neolithic Revolution.

In France, or elsewhere, kitchen-middens and tumuli (or mound-graves) provide evidence of this, but the most remarkable remains are the series of huge stone monuments which are scattered throughout Western Europe. The impulse to build these probably came from the Mediterranean area, but so many of the famous stones are associated with Brittany and western France that they are usually given Breton names. Thus a single-standing, upright stone is called a *menhir*; flat stones placed on top of upright stones form a *dolmen*; a *cromlech* consists of a circle of upright stones. But one should not think of these monuments as being in any way Breton. It has been pointed out that there are more megalithic tombs in the Aveyron department (in Dordogne) than in the Breton department of the Morbihan.

It was clearly a highly organized society which could produce these monuments. One has only to consider the many alignments of Carnac, which used to run down to the Atlantic, to reflect on the problems of finding a large supply of stones, of transporting them and of constructing them in a correct order. It was technologically a very advanced society, and it was a society compelled by religious ideas, probably the cult of the Mother Goddess, to construct these mysterious monuments.

It was probably between 1600 and 1300 B C that the first migration of Celtic peoples left the Danube area and invaded Switzerland and the regions of the Jura, Burgundy and Auvergne. A second wave of invaders probably coincides with the coming of the First Iron Age to Western Europe, from between

14

The alignments of Ménec at Carnac. Such mysterious rows of ▶
standing stones probably reflect a cult of the Mother Goddess.

This sandstone statuette (from Euffigneix, Haute Marne) of the first century B C wears the typically Celtic torc. The relief carving on the front has led to the suggestion that it represents a Celtic boar-god.

Gold coin of the Parisii tribe, first century B C.

1000 and 800 B C. Then between 700 and 450 B C they proceeded towards the west and the south-east. In the third century another group of Celts, the Belgae, occupied the north of Gaul. When, in 218, Hannibal crossed over the south of the country he met only Celts. The names of Gaul and Celt became interchangeable; it was in Gaul that they were most firmly established.

The Celts, however, did not form a unity. They themselves had arrived at different stages of their own development; they had mixed with the inhabitants who had preceded them, the Iberians (in the south-west), the Ligurians (in the south-east), the Greeks (around Marseilles). They were organized into a loose system of clans, tribes and leagues, living in different circumstances, with different customs, and acknowledging different leaders, frequently quarrelling amongst themselves and within themselves. If the total population, roughly within the limits of what is now France and Belgium, was about 8 million, then it seems that there might have been some 500 tribal units. They had a great variety of gods and we know the names of some 400 Gaulish divinities. Every tribe had its god, and although it would resemble the god of its neighbours, it would not be exactly the same. Gaulish culture must constantly have been changing: it was through contact with the Greeks that the Celts first learned the art of writing and the use of coins. Nor was there any standard physical

Left: eyes closed in death, grasped in a monster's claws, this stone head from Noves, Bouches-du-Rhône, shows Etruscan influence on Celtic art. Roman influence is more apparent in the carving (*below left*) of a boy holding a hare. *Below:* relief plaque showing an armed man and a snake.

That the Gauls were expert metal-workers is shown by this antique bronze cock from Lyons. 'Chanticler', the cock, is still the symbol of France, which could possibly stem from a play on *gallus*, the Latin for 'cock'.

type amongst the Celts. Classical writers must have over-generalized when they wrote that they were tall, blue-eyed and blonde. Archaeologists and anthropologists now find that there were many physical types, and it may well be true that a Roman emperor who wanted to parade his Celtic prisoners in Rome had to dye their hair so that their appearance would be as the populace expected.

Gaul　　What was common to the Gauls was their language, and their rural life. Caesar speaks of towns (*oppida*), but these were defensive forts rather than towns in the real sense of the word. It is true that they could be considerable in size; Bibracte (Mount Beuvray in the Morvan), for example, was 135 hectares in area, and was a commercial centre, with artisans and traders living there. Another *oppidum* in the Ardennes, when captured by Caesar, yielded some 40,000 prisoners. But this was an unnatural sort of urban life, since these fortresses were deliberately sited in inaccessible places. The vast majority of the population lived in the countryside and practised quite an advanced agriculture. The Gauls were expert metal workers and Gaul was renowned for its textiles. Communications were good and in the third century B C when the Rhône valley came into full use, it was possible to go from the English Channel to Marseilles in some thirty days. The discovery of the royal tomb at Vix, near to Châtillon-sur-Seine in Burgundy, reveals the wealth of a Gallic princess in the sixth century B C, and shows how valuables had been brought from very distant lands, such as Greece.

From the tomb of a Gallic princess of the
sixth century BC at Vix comes a
bronze *crater*, or wine-mixing
bowl. On the lid is a standing female figure
(*left*); below the rim a frieze of Spartan
warriors (*below*). The *crater*, made by a
Spartan craftsman, may have been a gift
from Greek traders in Marseilles to the local
Celtic chieftain.

In terms of social organization, too, there was homogeneity. There was a
nobility, to which people could accede through valour or favour; there were
a few slaves; there was the basic organization of the family, with an all-powerful
father; and there was the mysterious organization of the Druids, with important
educational, judicial and religious functions. It was the Druids who maintained
the oral tradition of the Gauls and who established the cultural unity of a
people who were politically fragmented.

Julius Caesar, young and ambitious, arrived in Gaul in 58 B C. In ten years of brilliant campaigning he conquered the whole country. Portrait head on a silver denarius.

Gallic war chariot. Silver denarius, reverse of coin opposite.

Rome had been an ally of the Greeks at Massilia (Marseilles). After the defeat of Hannibal in 202 B C, Spain became a Roman province and relations with Massilia therefore became vital for Rome. When, in 125 B C, a Gaulish tribe attacked Massilia, this threat to their communications caused the Romans to intervene and led to them annexing the Mediterranean coastline, which became the *Provincia romana* (modern Provence). Hardly had they done this when they had to face the first of the Germanic invaders, and they realized that they would have to establish themselves securely in Gaul. The story of Roman Gaul really begins with the arrival there of the young and ambitious Julius Caesar, in January 58 B C. Germanic pressure was causing an intensification of tribal movements and rivalries. Exploiting these internal dissensions, Caesar conquered the whole country within ten years. Only once was he seriously defeated, by Vercingetorix, and this had a dramatic effect, encouraging a momentary unity among some of the tribes. But in 52 B C Caesar defeated and captured Vercingetorix at Alesia (Alise-Sainte-Reine, near to Semur in the Côte-d'Or).

For the first time Gaul had a unified system of government. Roman rule meant colonization and Romanization. It meant the military and administrative effort that was necessary to give the Romans security. Soldiers and tax collectors were sent even to the most distant parts and a road system was built with extra-ordinary rapidity. Lyons, at the meeting-point of the Rhône and the Saône, founded in 43 B C, became the nucleus of the road system and the administrative capital. It also became a religious centre since it was there that the cult of the Emperor was established. Other cities were founded, or built alongside older Celtic agglomerations. Latin drove out the language of the Gauls, partly be-cause it was similar to Celtic, partly because as a written, technical language, it had many advantages. In any case, it was the language of the conqueror.

Roman civilization was highly sophisticated. Gigantic buildings were established for luxury requirements. The Pont du Gard was part of an aqueduct system bringing water to Nîmes from the region of Uzès. The theatre at Autun is the largest of the ancient world. There were probably some sixty-five amphi-theatres in Gaul, not many less than in Italy itself. Triumphal arches com-memorated victories. Great buildings housed hot baths. Rich landowners built themselves dwellings which were adorned with columns, mosaics, paint-ings and marble slabs. Everywhere there were temples, monuments, tombs, sculptures and decorations.

Vercingetorix.

A rich, sophisticated Roman civilization has left many traces in France. *Left:* funerary monument to a boy named Cocilius, who is holding a puppy. *Above:* mosaic of a hunting scene.

21

Great theatres, public buildings, aqueducts were as symbolic of Roman rule as the military roads. The Pont du Gard (*above*) brought water to Nîmes. The theatre of Orange (*left*) is one of the biggest Roman theatres still preserved.

The Maison Carrée at Nîmes (*above*) is
a perfect example of a small Roman
temple. Less well preserved is the
temple of Janus at Autun (*below, left*).
Below, right: the triumphal arch of
Orange, richly carved with battle
scenes and heads of conquered Gauls.

Romanized Gallic
warrior.

The success of Roman civilization has to be explained by the collaboration of the Gauls. Just as, during the conquest, Roman military intervention had invariably been solicited by some Gallic tribes, so now a large section of the Celtic aristocracy joined the Roman administration and even became Roman citizens. There were few serious risings against the Romans, although the number of Roman soldiers and settlers was always very small. The rich Gauls imitated the Romans and acquired large numbers of slaves, their sons went to Roman schools and the Celtic gods were merged with Roman deities.

But Gaul was too big and too backward to be wholly Romanized. Parts of the country, like Brittany or the Massif Central, escaped the full impact of Roman rule. Life in Gaul did not become municipal, for the Gaul remembered his tribe and did not identify himself with the city. As has often been pointed out, this is illustrated by the ultimate victory of the tribal name over the Roman city name. Thus it is Rheims (of the Remi rather than Durocortorum), Amiens (of the Ambioni rather than Samarobriva), Bourges (of the Bituriges rather than Avaricum), Limoges (of the Lemovices rather than Augustoritum). Celtic art did not disappear entirely; examples exist which show it persisting, or which show how its interest in decoration, for example, merged with Roman formalism. Parts of the Celtic religion also persisted; the goddesses notably were never absorbed into Roman mythology. In all these ways it is a Gallo-Roman civilization with which one is concerned.

Gallo-Roman stone relief showing two men hauling a boat laden with barrels (perhaps containing wine, to judge from the pitchers). River transport was much used in Roman times for heavy traffic.

Early Christianity had its martyrs in France as elsewhere. A fragment of decorated pottery from Tours shows a bound and naked Christian – identified as such by the Christ symbol of the fish – waiting as a lion springs from the right.

The origins of Christianity in Gaul are obscure. It first appears in the second century and seems confined to the south and to Greek and Syrian merchants. In 177 fifty Christians were martyred in Lyons; at the beginning of the next century Saint Denis was beheaded for trying to convert people in Paris. But it was in the third century that Christianity spread to many towns and that bishops were appointed. By the beginning of the fourth century Christians in Gaul were officially tolerated and the new religion spread beyond the towns to the rural areas. The Church in Gaul has two great figures, Saint Hilary of Poitiers, a theologian, and Saint Martin of Tours, a missionary (and the most popular of all the French saints).

It is while Christianity is growing that the decline of the Roman Empire becomes most marked. The fortunes of Gaul followed those of Rome. Internal dissensions, a decline in population and an economic crisis suggest a certain decadence, but it was the Germanic invaders, themselves displaced by invaders from Asia, who were the most dangerous. In the third century Franks and Alamans invaded Gaul which, the better to defend itself, constituted for a time a state independent of Rome. The danger was temporarily overcome but in the fifth century there were further and more spectacular invasions. At first it was the Suavians and the Alamans who roamed across France. Then the Visigoths moved into Aquitaine and in the course of the century they spread into the lands between the Loire and the Rhône and beyond, into Provence. With its capital moving between Toulouse, Bordeaux and Arles, their kingdom appeared the most powerful in Europe. In the east the Burgunds were in Switzerland, parts of the Jura and what was to be known as Burgundy. The Alamans were in Alsace, the Vosges and parts of Lorraine. Celts, fleeing from the Anglo-Saxons in England, came to Brittany. And after a temporary incursion of the Huns, the Franks came from the north and it is they who succeeded in establishing their authority.

There had always been a number of 'barbarians' in Gaul, brought there as slaves or as mercenaries, but the numbers involved in these invasions were probably not extensive. It was urban life which suffered most from their presence and the economy as a whole largely turned in on itself. Most of the invaders were Christians, although of a heretical branch. The Franks had been the exception to this and as they moved south under Clovis (465-511), allegedly descendant of the fabulous Merovech, their success was in part due to a change of policy. They were great warriors, but what counted was the agreements made with the Gallo-Roman bishops who had become the leaders of the towns. It was supposedly in 496 that Clovis was baptized and by this act he became the champion of the orthodox Gallo-Roman Christians. He succeeded in extending his

A ninth-century ivory carving shows Clovis, king of the Franks, being baptized by St Remigius in the presence of Queen Clotilde. Clovis founded the Merovingian dynasty.

26

The Merovingian period (c. AD 500–700) was noted for lavish jewellery and goldsmith work, such as this gold reliquary of St Maurice d'Agaune, decorated with pearls, garnets and coloured pastes.

power beyond the Rhine, establishing a united kingdom in Gaul, the *regnum Francorum*, and in founding the Merovingian dynasty.

With his death in 511 this kingdom fell apart and regional divisions became important. There was Neustria, from the Loire to the Meuse, containing important Gallo-Roman towns; Austrasia, a Frankish region stretching across the Rhine; the kingdom of the Burgundians; and Aquitaine, which remained very Gallo-Roman. The period of the Merovingians is one of wars and atrocities, economic stagnation, urban inactivity, artistic and intellectual decline. Only Merovingian jewellery and work with precious metals and stones has come down to us as particularly distinguished. Only the spread of Christianity, the increase in the power of the bishops and the growth of monasticism seem significant. Gregory of Tours (538–94), often called the first French historian, was particularly conscious of the decadence of his age.

It was a family of Austrasian chiefs which put an end to this. One of them, Charles Martel, defeated a Moslem force which had advanced from Spain, at Poitiers in 732. His son Pepin was proclaimed king of the Franks, anointed by the Pope and he united the kingdom under his authority. Then his son Charles, who became king in 768, united all the Christian peoples of the west under his rule. This was Charlemagne.

Charlemagne, crowned by the
Pope on Christmas Day 800, is
shown in a famous stained-glass
window from Strasbourg
Cathedral. The window, now in
a museum, was made about four
hundred years later, in a markedly
Byzantine style.

Charlemagne (742–814) is a figure in German history as well as in French, and when he was crowned by the Pope as Holy Roman Emperor in 800, he then appeared as the restorer of the Roman Empire in Europe. He was a great warrior who saw himself fighting for the Christian faith; he presided over a revival of religious, literary and artistic life. But it is not certain how real this empire was or how effective his government. We have to notice, for example, that he encouraged and even systematized vassalage, that is to say the procedure whereby a warrior would bind himself to a *seigneur* by personal agreement, and might in return receive the use of a piece of land. Charlemagne tried to ensure

Charlemagne's empire.

that the lords would similarly bind themselves to him. Thus grew up part of the system of man-to-man bonds which is called feudalism, and which was a move away from the Roman concept of state authority.

What is certain is that Charlemagne's empire was only temporary. With his death (814) it was divided up and the Treaty of Verdun (843), which separated France from Germany and Lotharingia, was an allocation of territories among his grandsons. France had new invaders. From the east came the Hungarians, from the south the Saracens, to the north-west came the Vikings who established themselves in Normandy. The king's power disappeared, the local counts and *seigneurs* became independent, the system of vassalage grew as men turned to the feudal rulers for protection. The monarchy became elective after 887, and a new family, that of Robert the Strong and his descendants, disputed successions with the Carolingians. Finally, the direct line of descendants of Charlemagne came to an end with the early death of Louis V. A descendant of Robert the Strong, Hugh Capet (938?–996), was elected king in 987. Although no one realized it at the time, it was then that the royal house of France began to reign.

Ivory cover of the prayer book of Charles the Bald, *c.* 870, illustrating the theme of Psalm 26, 'Judge me, O Lord'. By the Treaty of Verdun in 843, Charles, a grandson of Charlemagne, became king of the Western Franks, and thus virtually of what is now France.

Chapter Two

It is not easy to think of France, by the end of the tenth century, either as a country or as a society. Such concepts suggest an entity or a sense of wholeness. In fact, France was both divided and compartmentalized. Essentially France was rural and rural life meant local life. The population was distributed unevenly throughout the land. There were areas where the population was very thinly spread, and there were large regions of forest, moor and marsh which separated population groups one from another. Communications were difficult, and although experience shows that the extent of trade in early times was invariably greater than has been imagined, nevertheless areas which did not grow produce had little chance of purchasing it by the normal methods of commerce. Thus we find valiant attempts to grow wine in districts which were unsuitable, such as the valley of the river Oise or Normandy, because it was too difficult to bring wine from the localities where it grew naturally. And in all areas, what characterized society at this time was basic inequality. Adabéron, bishop of Autun, expressed the common idea, when he said that the clergy had to pray, the seigneur had to fight, and the servile class had to provide them with gold, food and clothing. Classes were sharply distinguished from one another and amongst a mass of people, suffering from under-nourishment, threatened by famine and desperately scratching a living with primitive instruments from a soil that was often poor, the seigneur lived in an island of wealth and leisure. Often his castle was badly built and sparsely furnished; by modern standards his life was hard, but because he was a seigneur he was supposedly endowed with qualities which excused him from the rigours that were inflicted on other men. His privileges were immense.

31

The gap between those with power and those without was considerable. In terms of the organization of authority, it is to local rather than to national units that one must look. Independent lords behaved as if they were sovereigns; the only difference between them and the king was the oath of homage which most of them took to the king as their overlord. And these local centres of power have to be divided into the various cultural regions. This variety was increased since certain of the regions had been more devastated by invasion than others. The Frankish influence was dominant in the north, and the Gallo-Roman region was naturally the south. The kingdom of Burgundy in the centre had proved a centre of refuge during the most recent invasions. To the west were the Celts of Brittany, who were hardly influenced by what was happening in the rest of the country, and the Norsemen settled in Normandy. In the south there was an isolated cultural entity, that of the Basques, and from the south came the influence of Islam. Contrasts between north and south have always been obvious. There is the contrast between the *langue d'oïl* of the north and the *langue d'oc* of the south; houses in the north tended to be built of wattle, wood and thatch, those in the south were of stone; the lands of the north have been described as the lands of hard feudalism, those of the south as lands where the customs and procedures of feudalism were imperfectly understood or rejected. But the contrasts between one part of France and another are more than these contrasts of north and south. All customs differed from place to place, and systems of land-holding, methods of cultivation, forms of collective activity, all knew a bewilder-ing number of local variations. Cutting across all these differences there was the Church. Its situation was privileged and its organization was becoming more sophisticated. It is an important element in the criss-cross of activities and responsibilities which filled French territory.

From the beginning of the eleventh century everything began to change. The population began to grow and by the end of the thirteenth century probably came to number (within the present French frontiers) something between 15 million and 17 million. Some have calculated that the French rural population by about 1320 was as dense as it was in the eighteenth century. This population growth was accompanied by, and has in many ways to be explained by, a revival of agriculture. There was a great renewal of activity. Forests were cleared, moorland was pushed back, marshes were drained. In some ways the French countryside began to take on its modern aspect. In parts of Normandy, for example, the forest had to be cleared by collective action. Dwelling-places

A fourteenth-century manuscript gives a vivid impression of the ▶ manners, comportment and costume of the time. It portrays (top left to bottom right) soldiers, councillors, clerics, peasants, artisans and merchants.

From the beginning of the eleventh century forests were cleared, marshland drained, and farming methods improved. Oxen were used for ploughing, and already the countryside was becoming a chequer-board of fields and hedgerows.

would be placed in line, each surrounded by a clearing; this meant that villages would be strung out over a long distance. But in parts of the centre, where it was a case of clearing away scrub, this would be done by single effort. A farmer would therefore clear a field and then mark its limits with hedges and bushes, so giving the countryside its familiar, chequer-board appearance. Often two villages would combine to clear the land between them, and perhaps a third village would grow up in this clearing; it might even today have the name which indicates its origin, like Neuville or Bourgneuf (indicating what is new) or Les Essarts (referring to the process of clearing the land). This extension of the cultivable area was accompanied by technical developments: wind-mills and water-mills became more numerous, the metal ploughshare and the mould-board were more widely used, the alternate sowing of winter and spring crops reduced the amount of land left fallow, the development of harness brought about a more efficient use of the horse. All these changes meant that more food was produced.

Town Life   At the same time there was a renewal of town life. This obviously had its effect upon the progress of agriculture since towns were making a demand for

Towns were thronged and busy. This Parisian scene (from an illuminated life of St Denis) shows boats on the Seine as well as traffic on the Grand Pont.

In fifteenth-century France, towns had paved streets with shops and a busy commerce. This street scene includes a tailor (his assistant in the traditional cross-legged posture), a furrier, a barber and an apothecary.

food on rural localities. Sometimes it was the old Gallo-Roman cities, which had never altogether lost their vitality, which provided the framework for renewed activities. Sometimes it was, as in the earlier period, the proximity of a castle or of a rich abbey which encouraged the growth of an agglomeration. But economic considerations, which had never been absent, now became vital. Towns flourished if they were well placed. Thus they could be on an important river and could serve as a port and a centre of distribution (like Paris or Rouen); they could be on an estuary (like Nantes); they could be on a point where the river was crossed (like Orléans); they could be placed at a point where forest and plain came together (like Chartres); they could have a rich hinterland, so that they were the natural centre for the bringing together and the distribution of some product (like La Rochelle for wine); they could be the centre of some specialized industry (like Limoges with its enamels); or they could simply be well placed, geographically, to have regular and well-established fairs (like Chalon-sur-Saône or Beaucaire). The population which went to live in these towns was mainly an artisan and a trading population. Because of this the rise of an urban population must have been limited. Often towns seem to have been

Fairs and markets are an early feature of developing towns. Here the bishop of Paris blesses the Lendit fair while, in the street below, a drover brings his sheep to the market.

From the eleventh century to the thirteenth, the Church played a prime part in the intellectual and spiritual renaissance of France. This miniature from the Chronicle of the abbey of St Martin des Champs records the granting of a charter by Henry I in 1067.

Education: a father entrusts his son to the monks.

divided into various sections, named after particular trades and occupations; sometimes there were deliberate limitations placed upon a town's expansion. In these ways the renewal of town life should be seen as a renewal of vitality, not as the growth of very large towns. Paris, with perhaps 80,000–100,000 inhabitants by the end of the thirteenth century, is already an exception. By this time France is a country of small towns and local capitals.

This movement, beginning in the eleventh century and culminating in the remaining two centuries, is often called 'a renaissance', and it is often explained as being the accomplishment of the Church. That is to say not only that the Church played a key part in the return to a vigorous economic and social life, but more particularly that the renaissance of the twelfth and thirteenth centuries found its real expression in the intellectual and artistic life of the Church. In the often quoted phrase of the monk Raoul Glaber, 'it seemed as though the earth were shaking off the rags of its antiquity and clothing itself anew with a white mantle of churches'. In many ways this is true. The process of extending the limits of cultivable land was encouraged by the Church, and when it was necessary to make a considerable collective effort, such as was required for draining the marshland and making and maintaining a canal, then it was often the Church, in the shape of Cistercians or other establishments, which was the principal force. It is also true that the Church was in strong and effective hands and most historians agree that at the opening of the medieval period a succession of churchmen were great politicians, reformers and promoters of the Church. If France was compartmentalized, the breaking down of the barriers and the interpenetration of the localities was to a large extent the work of the Church, and ever since the foundation of Cluny in 910, monasteries were the agents of this work. They were spread over enormous distances. They were not only centres of meditation and culture, havens for the exemplary Christian and agricultural outposts tilling virgin soil, they were also an organizing force and a source of action. Their churches were not only monuments to an established faith, they were also indications of a mentality which insisted upon development and experiment. Nothing is more striking than to list the great cathedrals and churches which were built and consecrated during the eleventh century in Normandy, that is to say in a region which had, at the beginning of the previous century, been annexed by 'barbarians'. The list would have to include the cathedrals of Avranches, Lisieux, Rouen, Coutances, Bayeux and Evreux, as well as the greater churches of Bernay, the Mont-saint-Michel, Jumièges, the abbey of Bec, St-Etienne at Caen and St-Ouen at Rouen.

Music: carved capital from Cluny.

The monastic life: monks at divine service (*left*).
Above: brother cellarer tests the restorative virtues of wine (from a thirteenth-century health manual).

37

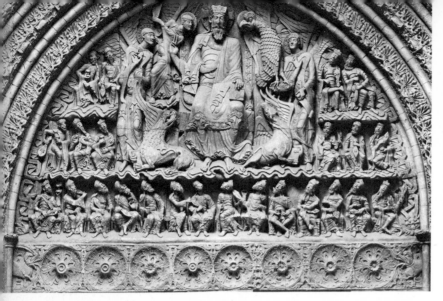

In the medieval churches –
monuments of an established faith
– builders, stonemasons and
sculptors worked and experimented
to the glory of God. *Left, above:*
tympanum of the abbey church of
St Pierre at Moissac, *c.* 1100.
Left, below: twelfth-century nave
of the abbey church of La
Madeleine, Vezelay. *Above:*
Isaiah, from a church doorway at
Souillac.

Right: ruins of the central tower, transept and nave of the Benedictine abbey of Notre Dame at Jumièges, Seine Maritime; tenth and eleventh centuries. *Below:* the cloister of Mont-saint-Michel, another famous Benedictine abbey, was completed in 1228.

But one should not give too much weight to the Church. Its effectiveness must undoubtedly have varied from region to region, and those areas which did not see vigorous and active church organization were not deserts of inactivity. As with most periods of time which have been given the title of 'renaissance', there is a danger of exaggerating the anarchy of the period which preceded it. And one should not underestimate the importance of certain events which fundamentally transformed Western Europe. There was the ending of the invasions into France and the stabilization and conversion of barbarians; there was the recession of Islam; there was the freeing of sea-traffic and the return of both the Mediterranean and the Baltic to being normal channels for the interchange of ideas and for trade. There was also the extension of the Capetian monarchy.

The Capetians Hugh Capet was only ruler of a small part of France, in the area known as the Ile de France, and in the north-east. He possessed a royal palace on the Ile de la Cité in Paris, but as lords who were frequently hostile to him owned the bridges across the river, he did not usually live there. He spent his time going from one part of his domain to another, and probably spent the longest periods of time in Orléans. Thus there was a vast contrast between his theoretical power, which extended south beyond the Pyrenees and north to Flanders, and his effective power, by which he was simply another feudal dignitary. It is some-times said that from the time of Hugh Capet onwards the monarchs attempted to unify their kingdom and to extend their royal authority by attacking the prin-ciple of feudalism. But to say this is quite anachronistic. The Capetians were themselves feudal lords and their policies were feudal. Their natural pre-

A section of the Bayeux tapestry shows William of Normandy ('hic Willelm: dux')
riding to join the invasion fleet, while behind him is drawn a cart loaded with weapons
and wine.

In a window of the abbey of St Denis is this portrait of Abbot Suger kneeling at the feet of the Virgin. Under his administration and thanks to his organizing ability and collector's zeal, the royal abbey became one of the glories of medieval France.

occupation was to control and to verify their own domain and to acquire further estates and this they did by all the well-established means used by feudal lords, such as conquest, marriage, confiscation, purchase, gift, legal subtleties and so on.

There were many difficulties for they had little in the way of organization, only possessing what was basically a household administration. The royal domain itself was threatened by brigands, there was trouble within their own family and some of their neighbours increased their power. The duke of Normandy, from 1066, became king of England, which not only increased his own strength and resources but which was to link England and France in a way to create complications; when the Plantagenets succeeded to the throne of England in 1154, Henry Plantagenet became Henry II and eventually inherited England and Normandy from his grandfather, Anjou and Touraine from his father, and Aquitaine from his wife. The count of Blois was another neighbour who increased his domains in a manner which was embarrassing to the Capetians. The duke of Aquitaine and the count of Toulouse were two of the princes whom contemporaries thought of as acting 'royally'.

But the French kings were moderately successful. They were lucky, in so far as they had sons; they were also well-connected and they were adroit rulers, in so far as they were cautious and careful not to be extravagant. They invariably had the support of the Church, which, rich as it was, needed peace in order to

Louis IX,
Saint Louis.

keep its possessions and further its activity. They continued the custom of anointing the heir so that the monarch always had a religious side to him. Then it does seem that there was some desire in France for an ultimate authority or arbitrator. This showed itself particularly in relation to the affairs of justice, and as the appropriate machinery grew up it became customary for those in dispute (especially the weaker party) to appeal to the king. The fact that the king did not pay homage to anyone, established him as a special person.

The progress made by the first Capetians towards unification was significant, although slight. It was the thirteenth century which was to be the great century of the Capetians. Philip Augustus (1165–1223) more than trebled the Capetian domain, notably annexing Normandy, Anjou and Poitou from the English and intervening in southern affairs when a heretical religion was flourishing there. After the short but ambitious reign of Louis VIII (1187–1226), it is Louis IX (1214–70), Saint Louis, who (at first with the regency of Blanche de Castille, his mother) was to have the greatest reputation among medieval French rulers. Devoted to the Crusades, he was also determined to establish peace with his European neighbours. In 1258 a treaty with Aragon gave France the right of suzerainty over Languedoc and Provence, and France abandoned all claim to any part of Spain. In 1259 he attempted to limit the extent of Plantagenet holdings in France and to define the manner in which they were held. Saint Louis actually handed over more territories than the king of England had held in Guyenne (a corrupt form of the name Aquitaine, which came into common use in the thirteenth century) but insisted that the king held it by liege homage. That is to say that he would have to send soldiers to the king of France and abstain from helping the king's enemies. This was an arrangement which was to cause great confusion, but it marked the consolidation of the king of France's authority as a feudal monarch.

Philip III (the Bold, 1245–85) inherited a monarchy equipped with institutions which enabled it to function smoothly. In 1271 his uncle, Alphonse of Poitiers, died on his way home from a Crusade, and it was claimed that his territory and that of his wife (who had predeceased him) should revert to the royal domain. Thus Languedoc, as well as Poitou and Auvergne, became the territory of the king of France. Philip also arranged for the marriage of his son, who was to succeed him as Philip the Fair, to his ward Joanna of Navarre, heiress of Champagne. Philip the Fair (1268–1314) did not succeed in his efforts to unite Guyenne and Flanders to his throne; however, he was successful in bringing a large number of fiefs into the royal possession.

Philip's three sons all died prematurely. Between 1316 and 1328 the succession was decided by a series of *faits accomplis* rather than by any proper law. In 1328 an *ad hoc* assembly of notables appointed the cousin of the last Capetian as king. Thus ascended Philip of Valois, rejecting the claim to the throne of Edward III of England, who claimed through his mother Isabella, daughter of Philip the Fair. By 1328 it could be said that the kingdom of France was the richest and most populous in Europe. The royal domain stretched over more than half of the kingdom. Brittany, Burgundy, Navarre, Guyenne and Flanders were the important areas which the king did not control, whilst in the south-west there was Roussillon which was an independent possession of the House of Aragon, and Navarre which was an independent kingdom, and in the south-east most of Provence still escaped the rule of the Paris kings. With such a domain the kingdom of France seemed to have a certain hegemony in Western Europe. In 1308 the Castillian ambassador said that the king of France was both Pope and Emperor within his kingdom.

There were many other changes taking place. The agricultural changes meant a form of relaxation of the feudal system. Labour services, which the peasantry performed in return for their holdings, were giving way to paid labour and rent. The French lords needed money if they were to go on crusade, or if they were to follow the code of chivalry. Just as castles were more expensive to build after the eleventh century, so the codes and customs of chivalry, whereby

Symbol of the power and wealth of the medieval aristocracy: Château de Fougères in northern Brittany. The moat is restored.

the Church tried to organize the practice of war in a way favourable to itself, involved the nobility in great expenditure. This aristocracy tried to keep together in a remarkably self-conscious way, with its coats of arms, ability to follow the profession of arms, cult of the literature and songs which recounted their feats in wars and jousting. But the decline of labour services removed one of the closest bonds of feudalism.

The nobility were also affected by the changes that were taking place in the royal administration. As the king's territorial responsibilities increased it was no longer possible for him to rule through hereditary officers whose activities were restricted to his household and his domain. Sheriffs (*baillis*) and seneschals were appointed to supervise royal and seignorial government, and soon another type of official (*enquêteur*) was nominated in order to supervise them, and sometimes an even higher official could act as a viceroy over a group of bailiwicks or *sénéchaussées*. The king's court became specialized, with a council for the actual process of government and with special sections concerned with revenue and with the administration of justice (the high court preserving the name of *parlement*). When the king required to raise special sums of money, then it was customary and convenient to try to gain consent for this. Thus assemblies were summoned which were known as Estates (*états*), and these were usually occasions for bargaining between the royal officials and the lords. Philip the Fair did summon a more generalized form of Estates, the Estates-General, when he was in conflict with the Papacy over the taxation of the French clergy; but such an act seemed linked to exceptional circumstances and hardly promised to be a basis for normal government.

Power of the King
It is obvious that the office of king was becoming more than the summit of a feudal pyramid; his powers could no longer be viewed entirely within the feudal framework. An idea of statehood, of a *res publica* which was not simply the property of the king, was beginning to be revived in France once again. The evolving machinery of government meant that an official class was becoming important, but there was an important corollary to this. During the eleventh and twelfth centuries the fiefs and principalities themselves began to develop their own administrations and to perfect their unity. Thus when the crown took them over it took them over as going concerns and consolidated entities. And this had two effects. On the one hand the crown was able to govern them and the state was strengthened. On the other hand the spirit of regionalism persisted.

Another new class which was coming into prominence at this time was the inhabitants of the towns, the bourgeois. It was natural that this class should

Stiff and stately, with their conventional entourage of priest and page, esquire and jester, the ▶
fifteenth-century nobility were conscious of their lofty position in the pyramid whose apex
was the king. This illumination from Froissart's *Chronicles* shows the author presenting a
copy of his work to the Comte de Foix.

Et me suis loyau
lement tenu à
parler des lo
outaines des
lontaines
marches mais les prochai
nes me ont este si fresches
si nouuelles et si endines
a ma plaisance que pour
ce les ay mises arriere

Mais pour tant ne serouv
noient pas les uaillans
hommes qui se esprouoient
a auanner es royaumes
de castille et de portingal
et aussi bien en gastouigne
en Rouergue en querin
en limosin en thoulousain
et en biforre mais biforent
et subtilioient tous les

find itself at odds with many of the characteristics of feudal society. These bourgeois were impatient with the mass of privileges, traditions and subtleties which they came across; they easily came together and soon had organizations for the protection and furtherance of their own interests. Perhaps it was natural, too, that they should come into conflict with traditional authorities when they tried to expand and protect their towns, administer their own justice and impose their own taxes. In some places, especially in the twelfth century, there were clashes between the towns and the *seigneurs*, whether the latter was ecclesiastical or lay. In the south, Carcassone, Montpellier and Nîmes are the examples of places where there was such conflict. But in many cases the towns were granted charters and in the thirteenth century particular privileges were enjoyed by a caste of wealthy merchants. In Champagne and in Flanders the movement of municipal prosperity was such that it was to the advantage of the *seigneurs* to grant these privileges. Elsewhere, the king of France was only too ready to show himself liberal, since he was continually looking for allies against his feudal rivals or against the Plantagenets.

It was not only the rich merchants who banded together. The retailers and craftsmen who were concerned with the same products formed their own *The Guilds* communities, the guilds. These associations were often united round a patron saint, but they were also concerned with control of quality and prices. They could bring together a variety of social grades, many of whom lived similar lives, but the humbler part of the urban population sometimes found itself excluded. Even where there were guilds there could be resentments and competition among the different classes. In the wool towns of the north there are instances, in the thirteenth century, of incipient social struggles.

While France remained essentially rural, the importance of urban life is clear. Towns could become centres of political power; they could be the seat of administrative authority; they could be places where money was most abundant. And, just as the wealthy patricians could pay for the decoration of churches or the construction of chapels, so the poets and *literati* of the time came to the town and deserted the wandering courts and the stultifying atmosphere of the feudal castle, where they were only expected to extol feats of arms. The towns became cultural centres (although many of them remained essentially seignorial in character).

The greatest of these towns was Paris, the largest of the western world. Political events encouraged this predominance, as southern areas looked more to the north and as the Albigensian heresy and its suppression affected the

Paris, greatest city of medieval Europe, was also the centre of royal administration. This illumination from the 'Legend of St Denis' shows the saint seeking admission to the city.

notables of the Toulouse-Carcassonne area. From the thirteenth century onwards Paris became the preferred residence of the king, who lived in his palace on the Ile de la Cité, or in the Louvre fortress, or at Vincennes, and Paris then became the centre of the royal administration and authority. But Paris was also a great commercial centre. The Seine, the success of the fairs in Champagne, the great conglomeration of crafts, luxury productions, food suppliers, moneylenders and bankers, made Paris a teeming city, a major factor in production, exchange and consumption. There, too, the schools had become the most famous in Christendom, to which students from all over the world came to study. The process of learning became organized into faculties and examinations. Buildings were put up to accommodate students; the students and teachers gathered themselves into a community, the University.

47

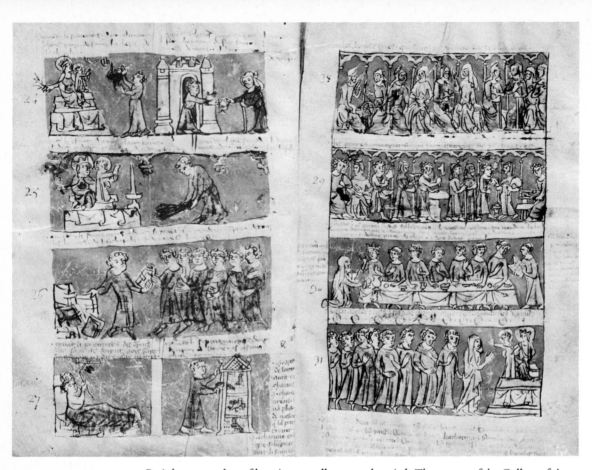

Paris became a place of learning as well as a royal capital. The statutes of the College of Ave Maria show students (blessed by their holy patroness) receiving a distribution of books, tending the collegiate aviary, and sharing other and more menial duties.

Perhaps Paris symbolizes the achievements of this period; at all events the influence of Paris and its region was considerable, and can easily be traced throughout France. Perhaps it is the Gothic architecture of the early thirteenth century which summarizes the nature of this civilization. It is to be seen clearly in Notre Dame and La Sainte-Chapelle in Paris; in later buildings in Chartres, Amiens, Rheims. It contains the ambition and the self-confidence, as shown by the upward thrusts; there is the lyricism of the stained-glass windows; there is the humanism of the sculpted figures. In this architecture, as in the literature, with such allegorical works as the *Roman de la Rose* by Guillaume de Lorris, as in the theology, there is a desire to reconcile things, to bring them together. It is a peak of achievement.

A peak of achievement: the upward-thrusting self-confidence of Amiens Cathedral (*below*), the beauty and the allegory of the *Roman de la Rose* (*right*), the humanism of the sculpted figures at Chartres (*right, below*).

Bowed with grief, survivors bury victims of the Black Death. Disease and famine cost fourteenth-century France perhaps half her population.

The fourteenth century was a period of disaster. The large population was a great strain on the resources of the land, famines became more frequent and by the middle of the century famine ravaged the country. It could be that from the mid-fourteenth to the mid-fifteenth century France lost between a third and a half of her population.

Disasters of War   To these disasters was added the calamity of war. Philip VI (1293–1350), faithful to Capetian principles, attacked Guyenne. Edward III, king of England and duke of Guyenne, claimed the throne of France. There were many French defeats, such as Crécy (1346) and the loss of Calais to the English (1347). John II (1319–64) was himself taken prisoner at Poitiers (1356) and the peace gave England a quarter of his kingdom. Within the country, the provost of the Paris merchants, Etienne Marcel, led a revolution against the royal authority, there was a peasant revolt and bands of soldiers roamed the countryside. Charles V (1338–80) with his Breton constable, Bertrand du Guesclin, recovered much of what had been lost, but Charles VI (1368–1422) was for nine years a minor; then he became mad and French reverses were a repetition of what had happened before. The butchers of Paris led a revolt (1413), the English won the battle of Agincourt (1415), Rouen was captured (1418) and in 1420 Henry V of England proclaimed himself king of France.

Above: the crowning of the young King
Charles VI (from the Chronicles of St Denis).
Right: with a brotherly kiss the king of
England does homage to the king of France.

pres le roy pre qui fu fil;
mons saint loys regna en
france philipe le bel son fil;
Et regna. xxvm. ans. Et co
menca a regner en lan de
lincarnacion nrc ihucrist apl cc.iiij.vj.
Et en celle annee al phors fil; du roy dania

Religion, loyalty, courage and the miraculous unite in the story – or legend – of Joan of Arc. When the English burned her at the stake in 1431, they created a cult.

Joan of Arc   It was then that the strange story of Joan of Arc (1412–31) took place. The main themes of the legend are well known. A very young peasant girl, convinced that she had been entrusted by heaven with a special mission, presented herself at the court of Charles VII (1403–61), the French king who was only reigning over a restricted part of the kingdom and who was known as the king of Bourges. She persuaded him to allow her to take part in the campaign against the English and their allies, the Burgundians. As a result the English were forced to abandon their siege of Orléans, which had great strategical importance, and Charles VII was able to advance to Rheims where he asserted his rights by being crowned in 1430. Subsequently Joan was captured by the duke of Burgundy, handed over to the English, who mounted a specially organized trial and who burned her at Rouen in 1431. She was probably nineteen or twenty years old.

It is easy to be realistic about the legend. We know that the English forces besieging Orléans were in a bad way, and that since the death of Henry V (1422) and the minority of his son, the English position had been weakening. We known that Joan did not actually command in the field of battle, and that Anglo-Burgundian differences might well explain the initial successes and the Rheims coronation. We know, too, that Joan's campaign was not the turning-point in the war; the turning-point was the reconciliation between Charles VII and the duke of Burgundy made in 1435, which enabled Charles to re-enter Paris in 1437. It is clear, too, that the English had every interest in magnifying the role of Joan and suggesting that she was an idolater and a heretic. Joan had simply become an instrument of propaganda and counter-propaganda.

But perhaps the real significance of Joan of Arc's story lies in its duality. On the one hand it is a banal episode in a period when antagonistic groups controlled the territory and when invasion and war had achieved a certain permanence. The episode of Joan is like a perverted form of chivalry, a mixture of religion, loyalty, courage and the miraculous. But at the same time the story of Joan of Arc has other depths. There is a sense of tradition. The king had to be placed in the same line as Clovis, Hugh Capet and Saint Louis. And there is a sense of nation. At her trial she is reported as saying, 'I do not know whether God loves the English or hates them, but I know that they will be thrown out of the kingdom of France.' It is not surprising that the subsequent cult of Joan of Arc should have coincided with the difficult periods in French history.

The last battle of the Hundred Years War was fought at Castillon in 1453, when the French army was victorious and proceeded to capture Bordeaux. Charles VII proved himself to be a good administrator, creating a regular army supported by regular taxes, reconstituting the Parlement of Paris, and he was supported by the richest man in the kingdom, the merchant and banker, Jacques Cœur. Normandy and Guyenne were conquered. Under Louis

Jacques Cœur placed this carving of a ship over the lintel of his house in Bourges – symbolic perhaps of the commerce that made him the richest man in the kingdom.

XI (1423–83), there are signs of royal absolutism. Surrounded by foreign and bourgeois advisers, he set out to destroy all opposition and to increase his revenues. His was the period of great annexations: Burgundy, Franche-Comté, Picardy, Artois, Maine, Anjou, Provence. It is a sign of the end of medieval France, that it is no longer a feudal kingdom, but a monarchy tending towards absolutism and centralization.

Louis XI – bridge between feudal kingdom and centralized state.

Chapter Three

The extent of the crisis that existed at the end of the Middle Ages has been disputed. It has been suggested that neither the Black Death nor the fighting in the wars were as extensive or as destructive as has been thought. Devastation was not spread evenly throughout the land, calamities were limited to a few terrible years rather than a prolonged catastrophe. There was rather a long period of depression which is to be explained by economic factors, such as an international shortage of precious metals. It is certain that the end of the Middle Ages was not to be seen as a return to the Dark Ages. Intellectual and artistic life in France did not vanish.

However great the suffering of unfortunate rural populations at various times, there remained important centres of luxury and of cultural activity. The court of France was, at least until the early years of the fifteenth century, a magnificent affair. Artists came from abroad to work at court or to work with the great dignitaries of the realm. One thinks of Jean and Pol de Limburg who illuminated the duke of Berry's manuscripts after 1415. France always profited from having several centres of cultural and artistic greatness, and although Avignon was outside the boundaries of the kingdom, the presence of the Pope there during the papal schism made this town an intellectual capital, and this had its influence. When the court settled in Bourges and started to live in central France and in the Loire valley, a number of towns benefited from this presence. A magnificent house was built for Jacques Cœur at Bourges; the Master of Moulins painted the triptych in the cathedral at Moulins; Jean Fouquet was born and worked in the region of Tours; the first châteaux of the Loire were constructed, such as Amboise. Burgundy was the most obvious example of a culture that was independent of the royal court, and the sculpture of the

Cultural Flowering

55

Chartreuse at Champmol or of Dijon itself, or the 'hospices' of Beaune, are monuments to this great period in Burgundian history. And Burgundy was not unique. There were many centres for the collection of tapestries and manuscripts, many patrons of artists, poets and chroniclers. The sense of progress and experiment was shown by the development of new architectural styles, typified by the 'flamboyant Gothic' of a church like Saint-Maclou at Rouen.

It is interesting to note what was happening at this time to the French language. By the middle of the fifteenth century, south of a line going from Bec d'Ambès, at the meeting-point of the Dordogne and the Gironde, to Limoges, Cantal, Annonay and Lautaret, French was never spoken, unless it was necessary to address some royal official. The popular language was the local idiom (*langue d'oc*) and the official language was Latin. In other areas, such as Poitou, Auvergne, Forez, or the region of Lyons, French had become

The fifteenth-century 'hospices' of Beaune, still fulfilling their original function of a hospital, are a monument to a time of Burgundian greatness.

Tapestries and manuscripts present a vivid picture of life in renaissance France. *Above:* an illumination from the *Très Riches Heures* of the duke of Berry shows the Ile de la Cité as it was then, with La Sainte-Chapelle and the old royal palace in the background. *Left:* detail from the 'Vintage' tapestry. *Below:* hunting, hawking and al-fresco dalliance in the Tournai tapestry.

the literary and the administrative language. From 1450 onwards French made extremely rapid progress. Before the end of the fifteenth century French had penetrated into Limousin, Périgord, the Bordeaux region, and the valley of the Rhône. From 1500 to 1550 French became the official, the administrative and the literary language of the whole of France. The *ordonnance* of Villers-Cotterêts, which in 1539 decreed that all judicial procedure should be carried out in French, probably only confirmed what had already taken place. Local languages became mere *patois*; the greater part of French people were able to understand each other.

This change is to be explained in several ways. There was a decadence in southern literature; French merchants from the north intensified their contacts with the south as the changing trade routes of the world increased the importance of the Atlantic sea-board. But there are undoubtedly two explanations which should be emphasized. The one suggests that there was a need for a new cultural development, however interesting and impressive fifteenth-century creation had been. It has been claimed that flamboyant architecture symbolizes the sort of dead-end which artistic creation had reached; over-ornate, over-complicated, it has been compared to the postlude of an organist who cannot conclude. The poet, writing for his courtly patron, became a mere *rhétoriqueur*. The printing press, established in Paris and in Lyons during the 1470's accelerated change. In a town such as Lyons, which by the beginning of the sixteenth century was almost rivalling Paris, and was an international centre of commerce and a meeting-place of ideas and influences, there was a new governing class which demanded a culture more in keeping with its practical interests. French became the language of medicine, science and history. There was a great movement of curiosity, learning and criticism which is called humanism.

The fifteenth century was a time of experiment and curiosity, of new styles of architecture such as the 'flamboyant Gothic' of Saint-Maclou in Rouen (*opposite*), and of the beginnings of observational astronomy, aided by such instruments as the astrolabe (*right*).

The second explanation is linked with this. The French language triumphed because it was the language of the king; French humanism progressed because of contact with Italy; it is therefore necessary to look at the reign of Charles VIII and his successors.

Charles VIII (1470–98) survived a troubled succession, since he was only thirteen years old at the time of Louis XI's death. In order to prevent Anne of Brittany from marrying the archduke of Austria and achieving a strategical predominance over France, Charles VIII had married her himself, in 1491. But the unity of the kingdom was not his major preoccupation. In spite of his own physical weaknesses he indulged in an extraordinary dream of conquest, which was to march upon Constantinople, supposedly to drive out the Turk and to win the imperial Crown of Constantine. The first stage in this procession was Italy, where he could lay claim to Naples through his great-grandmother. Therefore, abandoning Roussillon to the king of Aragon, giving Franche-Comté and Artois to the Emperor Maximilian, and paying vast sums of money to the king of England, Charles became in 1949 the first French king to set out on a war of conquest. A large French army moved rapidly through Italy but this success was soon lost in a welter of leagues and alliances. Charles VIII died in an accident in 1498, but his cousin, who succeeded him as Louis XII (1462–1515) and who also married Anne of Brittany, persisted in the Italian adventure until final defeat. Francis I (1494–1547) also had Italian ambitions. But these were soon merged into the greater rivalry that existed between him and the Habsburg Charles V, a rivalry that was further complicated by the diplomacy of Henry VIII of England and by the religious wars which followed upon the Reformation. Under his son, Henry II (1519–59), these feuds were continued until, in 1559, financial exhaustion and an increasing preoccupation with the religious question caused him to sign the Treaty of Cateau-Cambrésis with Philip II of Spain, son of Charles V. The Italian wars were ended, and largely to the benefit of Spain, since France had to give up Savoy and Piedmont, as well as many other towns and fortresses. 'Those who loved France', wrote Brantôme, 'wept at the thought.'

Thus France experienced some sixty-five years of largely uninterrupted warfare, at a time when all Europe was undergoing great changes. The institution of the French monarchy was naturally affected by all this. There is an interesting attempt to define the French monarchy in a treatise which was presented to Francis I when he became king. This was written by Claude de Seyssel, a

Louis XII (1462–1515) inherited vain dreams
of conquest and glory.

Savoyard churchman who had worked for the French crown. For Seyssel,
monarchical government by the succession of male heirs, as existed in France,
was the best form of government. The French monarch could only be a man,
so the kingship could not fall into hands which were foreign and alien to the
fundamental ideas of his French subjects. The French king was absolute.
But this did not mean that he could exercise power arbitrarily. He had to obey
the commandments of God. He had to respect the fundamental laws of the
kingdom (he could not, for example, decree that a daughter should succeed
to the throne). He had to accept the institution of justice, the Parlements, their
existence and their decisions. He had to govern through councils. In this sense,
the king was absolute within the sphere of his own authority and action.

It is obvious that such a theory of government, and Seyssel's contribution
is by no means unique, saw the monarchy as an agent which would preserve
the harmony of the kingdom. The king had both power and obligations. There
is the beginning of a complex system of legal checks and balances, traditions
and customs, privileges and obligations, which both strengthen and weaken
the central authority. Leaving aside a certain confusion concerning the exact
meaning of the word 'absolute' it is not surprising that historians should have
disagreed as to whether Francis I and Henry II were as powerful as any French
king ever was, or whether the monarchy of Renaissance France was usually
popular and consultative.

Francis I (1515–47), a king with all the graces. He added a new dimension to the monarchy and new territories to his kingdom.

But what is most striking is the fact that behind Seyssel's very realistic approach to the problem of monarchy is his assumption that France was not a mere geographical expression. There was a sense of 'Frenchness'. Other writers, too, such as Valéran de Varennes or Symphorien Champier, both of whom wrote at the beginning of the sixteenth century, believed that there were French national characteristics and qualities, that the French had a certain role to play in history. A popular poet, like Pierre Gringoire, could speak of the need for all peoples to have a God, a king, a faith and the law. It is as if he were pleading for the existence of something like the nation-state.

Francis I appears in history as a monarch with all the graces. When he succeeds to the throne he is young and handsome. He shows himself to be courageous by his victory at Marignano; he shows a sense of chivalry by requesting that he be made a knight on the battlefield by the Chevalier Bayard, the perfect knight and the bravest of the brave. A few months before his death a new Venetian ambassador reported him to be impressive, dignified, extremely regal. His court had always been brilliant; in artistic matters he was a connoisseur; he was a friend of scholars and poets. By his extravagance, his power

Marguerite d'Angoulême, queen of Aragon and sister of Francis I, presenting a book from her own hand to the duchesse d'Etampes, her cousin.

and his personality, he added a new dimension to the monarchy. Naturally such a character has given rise to diverse interpretations. For some historians he was simply a debauchee, whose popularity was greatly exaggerated; others have sought to find a progressive decline in his character; still others, while accepting his qualities, have refused to over-simplify in their interpretations of his reign.

It is certain that the territorial unity of the kingdom made progress during his reign; on the death of his first wife Claude, daughter of Anne of Brittany, it was clear that Brittany was an integral part of the kingdom. Because the duke of Bourbon sided with the Emperor who was then at war with Francis, his lands were confiscated after 1523. In 1525 the fief of Alençon was absorbed by the crown. In 1527 there was a move towards annexing the last of the great independent fiefs, that of the Albrets of Navarre, when Francis's sister married Henri d'Albret. This move towards territorial unity was accomplished by various administrative measures. The government endeavoured to increase its control over the provincial governors and the bailiwicks; the fiscal administration was reorganized so as to be more efficient; in the long conflict between himself and

Château de Blois –
the staircase tower.

the Parlement of Paris (which was a court and not a representative or legislative body), Francis was able to withstand the Parlement and even, in 1527, to publicly humiliate it by stating that it had not the right to intervene in affairs of state. By the Concordat with the Papacy in 1516 Francis gained extensive powers over the clergy within France, which were undoubtedly important. The Estates-General never met once during the reign of Francis.

But the monarchy had many weaknesses. In sixteenth-century terms effective centralization was an impossibility. Many decisions had to be taken at the local level. The monarchy did not have a large army and was dependent upon the support of the aristocracy. At a time of rising prices, the crown's revenue was inadequate for normal expenditure, let alone for his continual wars and personal extravagance. It was Francis who systematized the practice of selling offices. These were bought by wealthy families, who thereby tended to gain a monopoly of power. The provincial Estates continued to exist and to claim their privileges. The Parlements existed in many of the ancient feudal states which were part of the kingdom, and the Parlement of Paris, while humiliated, was not silenced. Francis was not always victorious in war, and

Château de Chambord – the Porte Royale side.

as the religious quarrels grew, he was not always able to represent any consensus of opinion. His attempts to extend taxation to the south-west caused a rebellion in 1542.

It is clear that under Francis absolutism had achieved a new consistency, but it was seriously limited. The wandering court, going from its châteaux in the Loire (Chambord, Blois), to its palaces in Paris, to Fontainebleau, had more in common with a medieval institution than a modern administration. Francis's successor Henry II (1519–59) extended France to the east by the annexation of Metz, Toul and Verdun, in 1552. But his death in a joust, in 1559, revealed the precarious nature of central government in sixteenth-century France, which the luxurious pomp of Francis I had concealed rather than cured.

One of the greatest of the French humanists was the man known as Lefèvre d'Etaples, who was probably born about 1450. Much influenced by Italian ideas and methods, Lefèvre applied himself to the study of the texts upon which Christian beliefs and traditions were based. Above all he valued the simplicity and the piety of the Fathers and in this sense his learning was devoted to a purification of Christian belief. It is therefore possible to speak about a type of

Fontainebleau – the Gallery of Francis I.

pre-Reformation in France since Lefèvre's work and ideas preceded Luther, whose writings did not start to reach Paris until 1519. Then in 1521 the Sorbonne denounced Lutheranism as heretical and the persecution of Lutherans had begun.

At first Francis was hesitant. He disliked the bigotry of the Sorbonne and he was anxious not to allow the Parlement of Paris to increase its reputation and power by becoming the champion of orthodoxy. He intervened to protect Louis de Berquin who had translated Erasmus and Luther and he admired the work of Lefèvre d'Etaples, who became vicar-general to the bishop of Meaux and who was supported by his own sister Marguerite d'Angoulême, the queen of Navarre. But Lutheranism spread quickly in France. Possibly because there was no tradition of heresy, and because there was widespread dissatisfaction with the organization of the French Church, Lutheranism became more violent in France and was associated with extremists, and with the destruction of images. Francis felt obliged to act against them and in 1535 the 'affair of the Placards', when the first direct attacks on the doctrine of the mass were posted up in Paris, and one was even fixed to the door of his bedchamber, confirmed him in his conviction that he could not tolerate this heresy. While

Sixteenth-century maps of Paris show the student quarter, then as now, centred in the Latin Quarter on the left bank of the Seine.

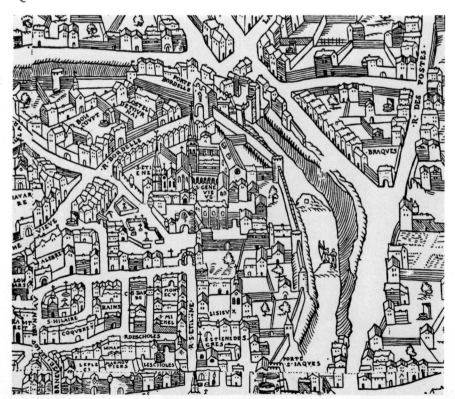

66

Near the end of his life, Jean Calvin was sketched by one of his students during a lecture.

another humanist who had clashed with the Sorbonne, Rabelais (1494–1553), became silent, in 1536 Jean Calvin (1509–64), a Frenchman born at Noyon in Picardy, who had taken refuge in Switzerland, published his *Christian Institutes*. This radical and severe expression of doctrine represented a complete break with Catholicism and the creation of a new Church.

Already in 1535 many Protestants had been hanged, burned and banished, and in the 1540's a number of long-standing heretics in Provence, who claimed to draw their religious inspiration directly from the Scriptures, were massacred. Under Henry II a special court was established for the prosecution of heretics, and in 1551 laws were passed against the Lutherans.

But the preamble to the Edict of 1551 had stated the simple truth when it had declared, 'the error grows from day to day and from hour to hour'. The number of Protestants in France continued to increase in spite of persecution. By the middle of the century it could be said that all parts of the kingdom were affected and that there were examples of Protestants to be found in all social classes. By 1558 Henry II was horrified to learn that the corruption had reached some of the greatest families. The Châtillon family, led by Admiral Coligny and d'Andelot, the king of Navarre, Antoine de Bourbon, his wife Jeanne d'Albret and his brother the prince de Condé, were important examples. Within the Parlement of Paris, formerly so determined in its opposition to heresy, there were now magistrates bold enough to show sympathy to the new religion. From Geneva ministers came into France and organized churches in

When Henry II died, his widow, Catherine de' Medici, acted as regent at a time of religious strife.

many different parts of the country. In order to establish discipline in the teaching, a national Synod was held in the Faubourg Saint-Germain in Paris in 1559.

By the middle of the century there was talk of some 400,000 Protestants, now called Calvinists, and by 1561 it was said that there were some 2,150 reformed churches or communities. It seems clear that the success of the movement has to be explained in many different ways. Sometimes there were areas, such as Provence or Languedoc, where Protestantism was a sign of hostility to a distant French monarch. Sometimes Protestantism attracted the distant, isolated, rural community, or it could equally prosper in an active or closely-knit urban community, such as Montauban. Sometimes the new teaching flourished in a cosmopolitan atmosphere, as at Lyons, but there is often a feudal side of the co-operation between country squires and the peasantry who jointly attacked the Catholic Church and the monarchy. Reform, both political and religious, could be the motive of many; while the Protestant ranks were also swelled simply by the discontented and those whom the economic and social changes of the time had rendered unsettled.

Protestant Success

The situation became critical with the death of Henry II, since his successor was a delicate boy of fifteen, the husband of Mary Stuart, Francis II (1544–60). He died after seventeen months, and the crown was inherited by his brother, Charles IX (1550–74), who was aged ten. During both reigns the queen mother, widow of Henry II, Catherine de' Medici, became prominent, but not

Henry III.

all-powerful. Around her three families fought for political influence, and their religious beliefs affected the political situation. These were the Bourbons, amongst whom the prince de Condé was the most able and the most ambitious, and a Protestant; there were the Guises, especially François de Guise and the cardinal of Lorraine, who were a powerful and rich family and Catholic; there were the Montmorencys, who were divided, since the nephews of Anne de Montmorency, the Châtillons, were Protestants. Michel de l'Hôpital (1505–73), who was Chancellor from 1560 to 1568, also tried to find a reasonable solution, and the Estates-General met several times. The starting-point of the crisis was an abortive conspiracy, organized by a Protestant called La Renaudie, which had the object of capturing Francis II at Amboise. The Guise family heard about this plot and, taking the initiative, massacred and imprisoned many of the Protestants.

It was in this way that the civil wars began, of which there were eight. Doubtless the damage caused by these intermittent wars has been exaggerated, but they were wars which were fought with great ferocity and which yielded little glory. It was a time of poison and assassination: the duke of Guise was assassinated as he laid siege to the Protestant stronghold of Orléans, Condé in

Henry III had a strong sense of royal display. Here, seated at the end of the left-hand row, he attends a ball in honour of the wedding of one of his favourites, the duc de Joyeuse.

Henry of Navarre, a Protestant, came to the throne as Henry IV when France, torn by civil war, was largely under foreign occupation. He became a Catholic before his coronation, for reasons of politics rather than conviction.

1569, then Coligny and many thousands of Protestants were killed on St Bartholomew's Day (24 August) in 1572. There were massacres in many parts of the country. When Charles IX died at the age of twenty-four, Henry III (1551–89) soon found himself at odds with the Guises. In December 1588 he had the duc de Guise assassinated at Blois. A few months later he himself was stabbed to death by a monk.

The heir to the throne was Henry of Navarre (1553–1610), who was a Protestant. By this time France was occupied by foreign armies; Philip II of Spain had the ambition of having his daughter proclaimed queen of France; while Guise's brother, the duc de Mayenne, had been proclaimed Lieutenant-General of the kingdom, the old cardinal de Bourbon was proclaimed king. Although he won several battles Henry was unable to enter either Paris or Rouen, and in order to break this deadlock and split the Catholic league he decided to abjure Protestantism. In 1594, having been crowned and anointed at Chartres (since Rheims was still occupied by enemy forces), he entered Paris. For four more years he had to fight the Spaniards, who were in Picardy and Burgundy. In 1598 they signed peace at Vervins.

Henry IV

FLANDERS

Calais

Meuse

Rhine

ARTOIS

Cateau Cambrésis

Somme

PICARDY

Amiens

Rouen

Rheims

Oise

Lisieux

Poissy

ÎLE DE

Bayeux

Caen

Evreux

Paris

Coutances

Seine

FRANCE

NORMANDY

Chartres

CHAMPAGNE

Avranches

MAINE

Orléans

FRANCHE-COMTÉ

BRITTANY

Amboise

Loire

Blois

La Charité

BURGUNDY

Bourges

Chalon

Saône

Rhône

Nantes

TOURAINE

Cluny

POITOU

La Rochelle

Limoges

AUVERGNE

Lyons

N

LIMOUSIN

DAUPHINÉ

Cognac

Bordeaux

Rhône

Garonne

Avignon

Nîmes

LANGUEDOC

PROVENCE

Bayonne

Toulouse

Montpellier

NAVARRE

Pau

ROUSSILLON

0 Mls   150

0 Kms   250

France at the end of the sixteenth century.

It is not easy to measure the destruction or the damage of these wars. Con-temporaries were apt to be extravagant in their estimates of the number of those who were killed, and accounts of abandoned houses and deserted villages may well reflect what was exceptional rather than what was normal. It seems that the wars took place at a time when the birth-rate was rising, and it is probable that it was periodical harvest failures which affected this birth-rate rather than the incidence of war. Nevertheless, it seems more than likely that the general rise of prices which took place throughout Europe between the middle of the sixteenth century and the middle of the seventeenth century, and which was associated with the coming to Europe of vast supplies of American precious metals, was exacerbated by the wars. Particularly as the French religious wars were wars in which foreign powers intervened, it became difficult for the supply routes to function normally. Generally speaking, the south of France found it difficult to get sufficient supplies of wheat, and many towns had to change their normal sources of supply. This combination of rising prices, shortage of food and war brought about many important and significant changes. The whole problem of government finance became critical; there was a strain on the resources of many, particularly nobles, whose incomes were relatively fixed; there was an intensification of population movements, with the normal seasonal migrations becoming lost in a movement of refugees, soldiers and destitute; there was a falling-off in the production of textiles and luxury goods as there was in the movement of trade; government officials, private individuals and the churches took part in a series of confiscations and of sales of land and property which, in some areas, became quite considerable.

But it remains difficult to generalize. Reactions seem to have varied from locality to locality. While it remains true that there was frequently popular resentment against hardship and against the inequality of suffering, it is not possible to describe any coherent social movement as the background to the religious and aristocratic conflicts. In Limousin during the 1590's there were peasant movements against the aristocracy and against taxation. In Brittany it was often the country gentlemen who led the peasantry against the towns. In towns there were often clashes which seem to have been class protests against capitalists or guild organizations. In other parts of the countryside there were movements in favour of peace and against all the religious leaders.

By the Edict of Nantes, April 1598, Henry IV guaranteed the Protestants freedom of conscience throughout the realm, liberty to hold public services wherever established and in one part at least of every district, absolute civil

First page of the Edict of Nantes, whereby 'Henry, by the grace of God King of France and Navarre' granted Protestants legal and religious equality with Catholics throughout France.

Maximilien de Béthune, duke of Sully.

equality with Catholics in all employments. The first of the Bourbon kings thus introduced a form of religious liberty into the state. He also employed councillors on the condition that they would serve the state. And as a realist he bribed the members of the Catholic party, who were still bitterly opposed to him, so that they would accept him. Such lavish expenditure made it imperative that the Treasury should recover from its bankruptcy, and he gave a modern aspect to his government by calling in Maximilien de Béthune, whom he made the duke of Sully (1559–1641), and who promoted agriculture and public works, improved communications and found it necessary to encourage industry with subsidies. Henry brought together an Assembly of Notables to ask their advice; he won the Parlements over to collaborating with him; he sought to establish his power by acting warily, tactfully and with calculated joviality. It is interesting to reflect that the man who emerged victorious from the religious wars was a mixture of high principle, cunning and carelessness. Like other French monarchs he was attracted towards projects of foreign conquest which were of doubtful value. These were ended when in 1610 he was assassinated by a madman, Ravaillac.

The winding frontier line of France had still not incorporated Artois, Cambrésis, the Bar and Lorraine (except for the bishoprics of Metz, Toul and Verdun), Franche-Comté, Roussillon and Savoy, Nice and the Comtat-Venaissin. The king was seen as the main element in government, accompanied by his councils, law courts and officers. There was no representative body which had any particular part to play in the raising of taxes, as in England, and Henry IV had never summoned the Estates-General. The movement of culture,

Henry IV, one of the most successful commanders of his time, spent much of the first ten years of his reign at war. In 1597 he besieged and captured Amiens, then occupied by Spanish troops from the Netherlands.

Pierre de Ronsard (*left*) and cardinal du Bellay, foremost figures of the literary renaissance, when Latin gave way to French as the language of learning and culture.

especially in the second half of the sixteenth century, had been literary as well as artistic. Whereas before this time it had been thought a necessity for learned works to be written in Latin, it now became normal to write in French. Many Protestants, after all, had refused to use a language that was not accessible to all. From different localities and from different conditions, a number of great writers emerged. Ronsard and du Bellay, who were the most famous poets of the group known as the Pléiade, belonged to the nobility. Louise Labé, who wrote sonnets, was married to a merchant from Lyons. Montaigne and Pasquier belonged to the middle classes, while Jean Bodin was a lawyer and the lively controversialist François Hotman the son of a judge. For the literary as for the political Renaissance, France was rich in variety, experiment and individuality. The time was coming when a uniformity would be imposed.

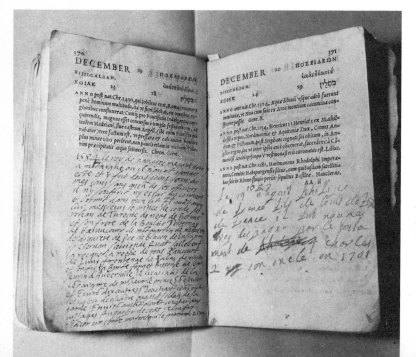

Montaigne's *Livre de Raison*, printed in Latin but annotated by him in French.

Chapter Four

Henry IV is supposed to have said, once he had accepted the Roman Catholic faith in 1593, 'France and I both need time to draw breath.' It has often been pointed out that his projects for rebuilding the city, which had been seriously damaged in the last year of civil war, essentially reveal a sense of order. He looked for a Paris which would be planned. The Place Royale (now Place des Vosges) which he had built was an ordered setting for residence and for public gatherings; Claude Chastillon's engraving shows a design for a vast semicircular Place de France, with eight roads spreading into Paris from this entrance on its north-east side. The poetry of François de Malherbe, who was particularly favoured

Claude Chastillon's design for the Place de France, Paris.

Nicolas Poussin, self-portrait. In art as in literature, a sense of discipline emerges.

by the king, showed a simplicity and a directness of language and metre which was a contrast to the more ornate poetry of his predecessors. Pierre Charron, the disciple of Montaigne (who had died in 1592), set out to organize his master's wandering, disordered thoughts into a coherent doctrine. When the architect Salomon de Brosse began to construct his châteaux, he emphasized the mass and proportions of the building, rather than its decorations. In terms of culture, therefore, as in politics, it is possible to talk of a sense of discipline replacing the restless ambitions of the sixteenth century.

But this should not be exaggerated. When Henry IV was assassinated his son, Louis XIII (1601–43), was only nine years old and the regency of his widow, Marie de' Medici, put authority into the hands of a ruler who was both a foreigner and incapable. The nobility and their retainers paraded in Paris demanding a return of privileges; the Estates-General was summoned in 1614 and all the orders presented impressive lists of grievances; great *seigneurs* like Condé and the duc de Bouillon (whose power was centred on France's eastern frontier)

Marie de' Medici, drawing
by Rubens. Henry IV's
widow, she ruled as regent
for her infant son.

threatened to raise the Huguenots against Louis XIII's marriage with the
Spanish Infanta, Anne of Austria. The time of assassination, conspiracy and
rebellion had come again, and war with the Huguenots and Habsburgs
increased the likelihood of royal bankruptcy.

Cardinal Richelieu (1585–1642), a younger son of a provincial nobleman,
who had naturally turned to the Church and to royal service as the sources
of wealth and power, became the chief minister in 1624. By this time the central
government had become much weaker and the opposition to Richelieu was
powerful. There was the '*parti dévot*', which wanted him to concentrate on the
suppression of Protestants and to be more conciliatory towards Spain; the
clergy, irritated by the alliances which were made with Protestant powers; the
intrigues of the court, especially those of the king's mother and brother, linked
to those of the nobility; provincial institutions, especially the Estates, which
sought to maintain their authority; the masses of the population, often so overcome by penury and taxation that they revolted against the state's authority.

Cardinal
Richelieu.

79

Louis XIII.

Against these Louis XIII and Richelieu presented a strange combination. The king, ill and neurotic, haunted by the fact that he had no heir until 1638, and Richelieu, also ill, but devoted and practical, were allies who frequently seemed on the verge of splitting up. Richelieu made little effort to reform institutions or to change the nature of administration. His main desire was to make things work smoothly, and in domestic policy as in his foreign policy it would be a mistake to see him working to any sort of system. He faced each crisis as it came, in spite of his clear principles.

Being himself a noble, he was not hostile to the nobility as such, though as a member of the smaller nobility he probably had his share of resentment against the great nobles. He thought that there were certain positions in the state which should be reserved for the nobility of the sword. He thought, too, that the nobility should form one of the strongest supports for the throne and he had a number of plans for making a special academy for young noblemen. But he was conscious of the power of the provincial governors, great offices which were usually given to the important nobles. They could not be allowed to behave as if they were great feudal lords, over-mighty subjects who could disrupt the kingdom, and he therefore deposed and executed those who were disloyal. He tried to put men whom he trusted, or his own associates, into positions of authority, and he occasionally used special agents and *intendants* for particular purposes. Thus it was that there was no thoroughgoing reform, and many of the nobility had an ambivalent attitude towards Richelieu, regarding him both as an enemy and as a source of hope. The nobility were not only divided among themselves, but also in their ideas. Did they wish to be military in their actions and functions? Should offices be distributed according to merit, to class or sold for money? The nobility was not sure.

A similar ambivalence persisted in Richelieu's relations with the Estates. He did not show any fundamental hostility to them, he was himself governor of Brittany and claimed that he wished the Estates to prosper. But the six *pays d'état* (Languedoc, Brittany, Burgundy, Provence, Normandy and the Dauphiné) were privileged to levy taxes at their own rate after receiving the royal demands and they paid much less than the remainder of the country. There were many conflicts with the Parlements, and Richelieu frequently claimed that they could not do or say anything which would harm the power of the throne. However, the Parlement of Paris continued to speak and to protest.

Thus it was that in Richelieu's domestic policy, as in the unceasing wars against the Habsburgs, part of the European Thirty Years War, we find no

Cardinal Mazarin, to whom Anne of
Austria, mother of the infant Louis XIV,
gave her confidence.

systematic clean sweep; so that when Richelieu died in 1642, followed shortly
afterwards by Louis XIII, and the new king was aged only four, it was not
surprising that there was a further period of unrest. The king's mother, Anne of
Austria, and the mysterious Italian to whom she gave her confidence and power,
Cardinal Mazarin (1602–61), soon found themselves at the centre of civil war
and more than once were refugees. These struggles were known as the Frondes
and they took place from 1648 to 1653. They represent a complicated imbroglio,
a struggle between the central government and the Parlement of Paris, between
the central government and rebellious princes, and they affected Paris and
much of provincial France.

There is a historical controversy surrounding this crisis in French history. *The Frondes*
There are those who believe that the Frondes should be seen as particular
movements of protestation, reactions to situations, and should be studied in
detail. On the other hand there are those who believe that in the Frondes there
was a constitutional movement, similar to the Parliamentary movement which
was roughly contemporaneous in England. Then there are those who believe
that the Frondes are only a particular expression of a seventeenth-century
phenomenon in France, that of peasant revolt which involved other social
classes.

The French population, still essentially rural, was periodically affected by
harvest failures, which appear to have had a direct effect on the demographic

evolution of the country. There were years of considerable crisis, such as 1618, 1630 and 1649. Harvest failures naturally determined food prices, and rises in the price of wheat would have considerable effects on the whole pattern of economic and social life, involving town as well as country. But these harvest failures were often local and rarely influenced all the regions at the same time. A more general price-change was the so-called depression of the seventeenth century, which probably started between 1620 and 1640, and which seems to have been caused by a reduction in the quantity of precious metal coming from America, as well as by a climatic change whereby both the winters and summers became colder. The years from 1647 to 1651 were years of catastrophic harvest failure.

Different regions of France seem to have experienced economic hardships at different times. Parts of the south were more sheltered from the crisis and it was not until well in the second half of the century that they felt the full force of distress. But in many parts of the country there was a constant popular discontent which could always explode into some violent insurrection. It could be that many of these movements were spontaneous and are to be explained simply in terms of poverty, fear and hunger, but there were other elements. Because, in this period, France was so frequently involved in the endemic wars of Europe, and because persecution of the Huguenots continued, albeit intermittently, there was an atmosphere of violence as well as the presence of armies, consisting of adventurers and of peasants who were still bound to their *seigneurs*

Peasant discontent is illustrated by this engraving of a foppish aristocrat receiving tribute from one of his peasants in cash and kind. 'The nobleman is the spider', the legend reads, 'and the peasant is the fly.' Crude though the presentation may be, the discontent was genuine, and gave rise to many disturbances. *Opposite:* fighting and barricades in Paris during the Frondes.

by conditions of semi-vassalage. Because of the wars, too, there was a constant rise in royal expenditure and an ever-pressing need to raise more money, so that royal tax officers were continually on the move. There was a general opposition to these officers. If the peasantry had to pay the royal taxes, then they would be less likely to pay their dues to the *seigneurs*. Even members of the administration who had bought their offices turned against the central government when special agents or *intendants* seemed to rival their power. Thus it was that peasant risings and artisanal disturbances were often incited or led by members of the nobility, or even by the bourgeoisie and office-holders in the towns. The accident whereby, on two occasions in the seventeenth century, the king of France was a minor and the Regency in the hands of foreigners, undoubtedly facilitated an alliance against the crown which was drawn from all classes. Not every rising or disturbance falls neatly into this pattern; that of Amiens in 1638, for example, seems extremely complicated. The rising at Aix-en-Provence in 1630, or in the Rouergue in 1643, provides a background of plague, severe taxation and high wheat prices, which is exploited by those who wish to emphasize provincial privilege and to preserve positions of individual benefit.

Thus the Frondes were the climax of a long crisis which was both political and social. The return to calm after 1653 was only partial, since 1658 saw another series of anti-fiscal revolts and in 1659 there were secret assemblies of nobles in

Louis XIV and his family. Even in such moments of ease he deliberately remained the epitome of kingliness – Le Roi Soleil.

different parts of the country, doubtless encouraged by rumours of the king's ill-health. Mazarin died in March 1661, and it was to avoid a crisis that Louis XIV, then twenty-two years old, declared that he would be his own first minister and decisively took over the government.

Most accounts of the long reign of Louis XIV (1638–1715), who legally reigned for seventy-two years, emphasize the man and the court. He was to become the epitome of kingliness, the extreme example of the ruler who had no private life but who spent all his time devoted to the business of being the ruler. Naturally there is a great contrast between the young, energetic and self-confident monarch and the aged and sick old man, whose death led to singing and scurrility in the Paris streets, and there is little similarity between the extravagant court of the early years and the sad, morose court dominated by Madame de Maintenon. However, the link is there. From the beginning, the laws of etiquette and ceremonial obliged the king to live a life of perpetual parade, but they served to demonstrate his great superiority over all those who

'The King, alone, governing his realm.' The symbolism, though fairly simple, speaks the truth: Louis XIV remained the ruler to the end of his long reign.

Jean-Baptiste Colbert – in the centre of this group mounted on conventionally cavorting horseflesh – was, after the death of Mazarin, much the most able of Louis XIV's ministers.

attended him. Within a few days of his death, and too ill to do more than take a little liquid, he presided over a great banquet; council was held from his bed. There was no deviation from ritual: the court and the government had to revolve around the king. He was an absolute monarch, whose power was not shared by any individual, such as a first minister or a mistress, or by any institution, such as a Parlement or the Estates-General.

In spite of the unity imposed on this long period by the personality and will of the king, the reign cannot be considered as a single period. From the time of his effective government, various divisions have been suggested. At first there was the period up to 1664, when the king affirmed his power, when the Dauphin was born, and when the Superintendent of Finances, Fouquet, was disgraced. It was from about 1664 that the administrative monarchy began to be organized and the great reforms of Colbert began to take shape. The Parlements were ordered to register edicts without alteration; the laws were codified in a series of ordinances; the army was made more dependable; the *intendant*, who had been established by 1635 but later withdrawn, from being a kind of inspector undertaking an exceptional task, was made into a regular feature of the administration; the detailed regulation of industrial production got under way. After 1672 there were some changes. This was the time of the war against

Much the most influential of Louis's mistresses was Madame de Maintenon, who became his wife after the queen died.

Holland and of war against the first European coalition. There was already a sense of turning to expedients rather than ensuring reforms. After 1678 there was the quarrel with the Pope, but then the king became more austere. Colbert died in 1683 and his successors never had the same influence. After the death of the queen, Louis married Madame de Maintenon, intensified his persecution of the Jansenists* and Huguenots and organized his crusade

* A sect within the Catholic Church which was regarded as heretical because of its insistence on predestination for salvation.

against Algiers. After 1686 there was a period of twenty-four years of war, the most important that Europe had yet known. Louis was gradually moving towards a form of capitulation and negotiation, giving up his quarrel with the Pope, giving up his hope of ruling the Low Countries, giving up the ambition of acquiring the whole of the Spanish inheritance and entering into new difficulties at home.

It has been argued that Louis XIV's reign was a great façade. Just as the king himself used to wear blocked shoes, to give the impression of height, so he has deceived historians with his splendour. In reality, much of the government was carried out by Colbert and Le Tellier, who fostered the illusion that it was the king who took all the decisions. Equally it can be argued that there were no great institutional changes. The administration soon found the limits of its efficacity when officials, often with little experience, came into conflict with local notables, conscious of their privileges and of local support. The financial crisis of the monarchy became acute by the end of the reign, and no satisfactory method of raising money was devised. From 1700 onwards government became a matter of expedients and improvisation. Commerce and industry were stagnating; there was famine and plague. There was widespread criticism of the king, so that Archbishop Fénelon could call France 'a great poorhouse, desolated and provisionless'. There was open defiance, revolt, and a breakdown of order, and Louis was in dispute with the Parlement of Paris when he died.

And yet there had been accomplishments. At the beginning of the reign there had been a continuation of popular, anti-fiscal risings, so that in 1673, for example, Bordeaux was in the hands of the mob for a considerable period of time and it was said that the government had had its greatest defeat since the time of the Frondes. But there is evidence which suggests that by the end of the reign there had been a significant change in the nature of agitation. The urban authorities and the bourgeoisie no longer joined or encouraged insurrection and a greater solidarity seemed to exist between them and the crown. Possibly the bourgeoisie was more conscious of economic difficulties, but it is as if what separated it from the crown was no longer as important as what united it to the crown. The monarchy of Louis XIV had tried to draw together the interests of the whole country. Through his marriage with Maria Theresa of Spain Louis hoped to achieve a great inheritance when the king of Spain died without heirs; thus the dynasty was identified with the frontiers and the interests of France. By his economic policy, Louis XIV wanted France to

In spite of the administrative advances of Louis XIV's reign, plague and pestilence persisted. A contemporary engraving ('drawn on the spot, during the plague of 1720') shows that even the better quarters of Marseilles were not immune.

acquire wealth; by his religious policy he aligned his rule to the cause of the Catholic Church; by his court policy he sought to occupy the over-mighty subject; and by his administrative policy and his own industrious application, he tried to make the system work more efficiently. *Intendants* stayed in their areas for longer periods; government became more technical and more organized. Thus the royalty attempted to make itself a sort of amalgam of different aspirations. Where there seemed to be deviations, such as Protestantism and Jansenism, then the machinery of state was called in to suppress them. Louis XIV may never have said, 'L'Etat, c'est moi', but on his death-bed, he did say that he was departing, yet the state remained.

It was the effectiveness of government which enabled Louis to raise great armies and to win his military victories. He inherited from the diplomacy of Richelieu and Mazarin a situation which put an end to the encirclement of France. It did not seem that the Habsburgs of Austria and Spain were in such a strong position to invade and partition France. Louis strengthened his frontiers in the north-east by gaining Artois, in the east Alsace and Lorraine, in the south Roussillon and Cerdagne. Later he was to take areas in the Spanish Netherlands, in Franche-Comté, and in Alsace (Strasbourg became French in 1681). Although the Treaty of Utrecht (1713) represented some loss

comme les Negres
rament de bout

Commerce
des Esclaves

The acquisition of colonies, dating from Champlain's
opening up of 'Nouvelle France' in North America a
hundred years before (*below*), was encouraged by
Richelieu and Colbert. The trade thus stimulated (*left*)
was profitable.

As the colonial empire grew, so did
the home ports. The prosperity of
Rouen (*above*) and Dieppe, derived
from commerce and shipping, dates
from the early eighteenth century.

of territory that had earlier been acquired, the France of 1713 was clearly greater
than the France of 1610 and her frontiers were endowed with a formidable
collection of fortresses. The acquisition of colonies, which had been encouraged
by Richelieu and Colbert, meant that France possessed vast territories in North
America, as well as important trading counters in Africa and India and
colonies in the West Indies. The colonial trade was extremely profitable, and
as merchant ships improved, ports such as Bordeaux, Nantes, Rouen and
Dieppe had a promising future.

If the sixteenth century had been the century of Italian cultural influence,
from the middle of the seventeenth century there was a great assertion of French

DISCOURS
DE LA METHODE,
Pour bien conduire fa raison, & cher-
cher la verité dans les Sciences.
PLUS
LA DIOPTRIQUE
ET LES METEORES,
Qui font des effais de cette METHODE.
PAR RENE' DESCARTES.
Nouvelle Edition, revûë & corrigée.

A PARIS,
Chez GABRIEL AMAULRY, Place de
Sorbonne, à l'Annonciation.

M. DCC. XXIV.
AVEC PRIVILEGE DU ROY.

When Descartes, seeking peace and quiet
in order to think, lived in Haarlem, Frans
Hals painted his portrait. His *Discours de
la Méthode*, quintessence of French
intellectual organization and scepticism,
demonstrated that the French language was
suitable for scientific discussion.

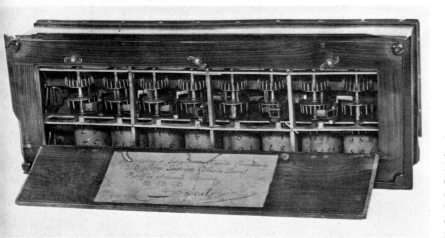

The first computer? This
calculating machine, invented by
Blaise Pascal about 1644, works
on the same principle as a motor-
car distance meter. Each ten-cog
wheel moves the next one on by
one cog for each complete
revolution.

cultural importance. Descartes (1596–1650) and Pascal (1623–62) demonstrated that the French language was suitable for scientific discussion. French began its career as the language of diplomatic treaty. The influence of French writers, whether of theatrical authors, theologians or novelists, was considerable. The architecture of Versailles and its gardens was imitated throughout Europe. The *rayonnement* of France had never been so great.

It was true that not all this could be attributed to Louis XIV. Wherever his personal opinions were important, as in the persecution of Protestants and Jansenists, then it could be said that his influence was disastrous. Most of the great figures of seventeenth-century classicism had started their careers before Louis's personal rule had begun. It has been suggested that in the latter years of the reign a depressing uniformity was setting in, as instanced in the interior decorations of Versailles. But the great criticism of the reign is that there had been no institutional change; absolutism had been reinforced, but the complexities of the existing social structure remained.

Jean Racine (*above*). *Left:* Molière, actor as well as playwright, as Caesar in Corneille's *La Mort de Pompée.*

Versailles – a supreme
expression of French
power and influence.

Left: Louis XV, by Van Loo: an indecisive monarch.
Right: Madame de Pompadour, by Boucher; the king's mistress.

When Louis XIV died, he was succeeded by his great-grandson, aged five. There had to be another Regency, but this time history did not repeat itself. The provisions in Louis XIV's will for a Regency Council and for a privileged position to be given to his illegitimate son were defied, and the duke of Orleans acted as Regent until 1723. After his death it was the duke of Bourbon who controlled affairs, and after his disgrace in 1726 it was Cardinal Fleury. There was no return to Frondes and there was no disruption of the kingdom.

Louis XV   Louis XV (1710–74) does not seem to have had any particular ambition. After Fleury's death in 1743 he decided to be his own chief minister, but he had little energy for administrative work and he has often been represented as showing indifference to most matters except for women and hunting. He preferred the appearance of power rather than the reality, and although the political influence of favourites such as Madame de Pompadour should not be exaggerated, there was a tendency for policies to change for no very good reason, or for government to oscillate between firmness and indecision, which betrayed an inadequate ruler.

If the king and the great nobility were showing a reluctance to stir themselves, the same could not be said about the Parlements and the nobles who had come to dominate these courts. The habit of selling judicial posts and with them the privilege of hereditary nobility meant that the Parlements had become the bulwarks of the *noblesse de robe*. Throughout the eighteenth century the Parlements were to insist on their rights, and the situation was given a particular edge when the Parlements became the defenders of the Jansenist sect within the Catholic Church.

As government became more complicated so the king's ministers became, in practice, more independent. It has sometimes been said that the king could only control a minister by dismissing him. It became increasingly difficult to estimate where power lay in reality, although in theory it was the king who was always supreme. It is equally difficult to say where power lay in the provinces. The *pays d'état* did not always possess active assemblies. In most of France the *intendants* were given authority by the king to watch over other officers, to maintain order and justice, to promote prosperity and raise money. It has often been said that France in the eighteenth century was ruled by thirty *intendants*, but it was not as simple as this. In many cases the *intendant* had to fit in with the notables of the province; he was not always supported by the king, he was not the only representative of monarchy and he was often dependent upon a host of officials who had purchased their positions.

Thus there was confusion at the centre and at the periphery. The French monarchy had once been essentially judicial; French absolutism, as seen by many, had come to exist in order to ensure that there was peace and order at home and that wealth could increase. But this meant that the monarchy had become administrative, and it was becoming increasingly difficult for this administrative machine to function effectively within the existing social structure. Nothing highlighted this difficulty more than the financial question.

From about 1730 a long-term rise of prices got under way again. This meant that the expenses of government were considerably increased. At the same time it was impossible for the French government to avoid taking part in the European wars of the eighteenth century. It has been said that there were two wars within the various conflicts, often dynastic in origin. There was the war for the mastery of the seas and for overseas possessions; and here it was

England that was the victor. Then there was the war for mastery of the continent and here it was Prussia and Russia which appeared as the strong powers. It was only France which took part in both wars. In the first war France lost Canada and India, and in the second France gained little. Confidence in the government was shaken for many. And the growing military and naval expenditure had to be met.

If the government was in financial difficulties the country was not poverty-stricken. A rising population meant rising demand; rising prices meant rising profits. The producing classes prospered. It has been estimated that there was an average annual rate of growth in Bordeaux of 4 per cent in the course of the century. Such growth came in uneven periods of development; boom was followed by depression. But it was natural that the crown should wish to profit from the prosperity that surrounded it and that it should wish to increase taxation among those who were rich. This meant an assault on privileges, and a tussle with the Parlements.

In the 1760's there was a dispute between the king on the one hand and the Estates of Brittany and the Parlement of Rennes on the other, because the governor had tried to increase taxes in order to carry out a road-building scheme. There was a flurry of resistance in the Parlements to an attempt to maintain war-time rates of taxation after the Seven Years War had ended in 1763. In 1766 the king asserted his sovereign power and denied that the magistracy formed any special order, saying that the magistrates were simply his officers. In 1771 the financial deficit was so alarming that the government was forced to take action and with Maupeou as Chancellor the Parlements were abolished and new courts established; the sale of judicial offices was stopped and the judges were to be appointed and paid by the crown. With the Parlements out of the way, financial reforms were initiated and a new assessment of income was undertaken.

This was a sort of *coup d'état*. It aroused tremendous opposition. There was a great outcry from all those who were privileged and who thought that they would have to pay more in taxes under the new system. The king was attacked as a tyrant. It was claimed that the 'natural rights' of citizens had been violated. Many writers joined in the protests. Eventually the Parlement of Paris followed the traditional action of calling out the mob in Paris in order to attack the new courts. It was not surprising that when Louis XV died in 1774, his grandson Louis XVI (1754–93) immediately gave way to pressure, dismissing Maupeou and recalling the Parlements. It was an admission of failure by the crown.

Building a road, painting by Joseph Vernet, 1774. The tax-raising made necessary by schemes like this led to resistance, and to attempts at reforming the tax system.

Thus the financial crisis of the crown revived an old-standing administrative crisis, and behind this lay a social situation which was later to explode. It has sometimes been argued that the nobility considered themselves to be a class apart from the others. They were exempt from the land-tax at a time when they were becoming much more effective as a class. It is said that the nobility were working together, the *noblesse d'épée* along with the *noblesse de robe*; they were marrying into the rich bourgeois families, exploiting their estates, collecting their feudal dues. Against this nobility the rising wealthy bourgeoisie showed its resentment at having its enterprise continually blocked. It is claimed that as the bourgeois grew in numbers and in wealth, they were increasingly conscious of the injustice of aristocratic privilege. Eighteenth-century towns in particular, resenting the continuous efforts of the administration to exact more money from them, asked why the nobility and the clergy should be exempted from general taxation.

It has also been argued that large numbers of the nobility were, in fact, very poor. The provincial nobility were obliged to be thrifty. Nor is it true to say that they were exempted from taxation. They paid an income tax, the *vingtième*, and there were many rich bourgeois who also enjoyed certain fiscal privileges or who were able to evade taxation. It has been argued that the distinctions between nobility and bourgeoisie should not be exaggerated for there were many bourgeois who purchased land and who enforced their feudal rights. Attempts by Parlements to restrict certain office-holders to members of the nobility were not as annoying as they might seem, because they could always be waived in certain circumstances, just as rich men could always purchase a false genealogy.

Gathering Crisis

Le Nain's *Return from the Christening*:
plain living for the peasantry.

Thus the fundamental social issue was that between rich and poor, made all
the greater by the fact that there was no agrarian revolution in France. The
mass of the population were peasants, and although there was necessarily
variation in their conditions, there were millions whose small-holdings were
inadequate for their needs, or who were forced to join the swelling numbers of
labourers working on other men's lands. The population in the towns was

Fragonard's *The Swing*:
high-flying luxury for the
fortunate few.

increasing and all those who had to buy food suffered from rising prices and from the catastrophic conditions which could accompany a poor harvest.

This seemed all the worse when the government's failure to deal with the nation's problems appeared so obvious. It is in these circumstances that the movement of thought which is called the Enlightenment has to be studied in France. These thinkers were most influenced by the scientific knowledge and awareness of the world which had been growing since the seventeenth century, but they were also influenced by the conditions in which they found themselves. There were a profusion of customs and laws, traditions and regulations, which caused uncertainty, injustice and inefficiency. As Voltaire said, in France you changed the system of law as you changed post-horses. Perhaps it is because it was in France that there was most clearly this confusion of the corporative, the hierarchical and the paternalistic, that the Enlightenment was most famous in France. The *philosophes* believed that the laws should rule; they asserted that the individual has certain rights; they believed in equality, including equality before the law; they believed in liberty, including economic freedom; they attacked the traditions, superstitions, assumptions on which French society was based; they thought of the community as a whole. Although the Enlightenment in France consisted of a series of individuals who were very different one from another, they together constituted a formidable challenge to the existing social and political order. It is natural that their role has always been considered important in shaping the revolution that was to develop.

Jean-Jacques Rousseau.

The Enlightenment

An assembly of *philosophers* – the thinkers of the Enlightenment. Numbers on this engraving aid identification of (1) Voltaire, (4) d'Alembert and (6) Diderot.

Louis XVI. This portrait by Ducreux was painted in prison, three days before the king's execution. Although aged thirty-eight, he appears much older.

It could be said that in 1774 all the elements were present which are to be associated with Revolution. The new king, who was only twenty years old, was a man with the best of intentions, but he had a very confused idea of what should be done. The government demonstrated that it had abandoned Maupeou's reforms, since the Parlements were recalled; but a known reformer, Turgot (1727–81) was appointed controller-general and the *philosophes* were delighted. Outside governmental circles a far vaster change was beginning to make itself felt; the population had been steadily rising (by the end of the century it was to number about 26 million) and the pressure on supplies was growing greater. A succession of bad harvests (1770, 1772 and 1774) led to high prices and exhausted the reserves of both peasants and workers. Turgot, faithful to his principle of removing all natural obstacles to man's economic activity, decreed that there should be free trade in grain. (This probably led to a further increase in prices since it encouraged speculators to sell where the prices were highest.) By the spring of 1775 there were riots in several different parts of France, including Paris, and although these risings were spontaneous protests against high prices, there was also a tendency to blame Turgot and his measures. At the same time, there were those who believed that 'the flour war', as these disturbances were called, had been fomented by Turgot's opponents. Thus there is administrative confusion, violence, fear, misunderstanding and rumours of conspiracy: all the elements which were to recur in 1789.

Turgot was not destined to remain in power for long. In 1776 he issued his Six Edicts which would have converted labour services into a money tax to be paid by all landowners, abolished the guilds and freed the internal grain trade. The Parlement of Paris refused to register these decrees, which were clearly attempts to raise money by increasing economic activity, but which were also attacks on privilege. Their remonstrance refused the indiscriminate confusion of all the orders in the state being submitted to a uniform land-tax. The king gave way and Turgot was dismissed.

Louis XVI was unfortunate, since his reign coincided almost exactly with the economic depression. There was a slackening of commercial activity, a decline in productivity, a rapid rise in unemployment. A fall in prices over a period of some ten years hit all those classes whose revenues were derived from land, thus making it all the more difficult to increase taxation. It also meant that the business community was in no position to consider any repudiation or refunding of the government's debts.

The fact that France joined in the American War of Independence, from 1778 to 1783, intensified the crisis by adding a new load to the debt. An association was formed, even at a long distance, between the French and a state which had broken with the past and started afresh, according to the principles of reason and humanity. In France, when the Swiss banker Necker (1732–1804) was controller-general, from 1771 to 1781, the financial difficulties were met by a policy of loans, but when Calonne (1734–1802) became controller-general in 1783, he summoned an Assembly of Notables in the hope that they would approve schemes for a reform in taxation. They rejected his plans, but the fact remained that an absolute monarch had thought it necessary to consult with an Assembly which had some claim to represent at least part of the nation. The idea began to be put about that the Estates-General, which had last met in 1614, should be summoned. La Fayette (1757–1834), who had fought for the Americans, was among those who proposed this.

The first cross-Channel balloon: Blanchard and Jeffries, 1785.

As before, a fiscal issue was becoming an institutional crisis. The Parlements refused to register decrees for new taxes and in May 1788 they had their powers of verifying laws and taxes taken from them. A new court was established which would have been a permanent Assembly of Notables, while legal reforms removed many of the seignorial judicial powers. The result was widespread resistance throughout France. In towns where there were Parlements, the magistrates brought the mobs out; where there were Estates, they met and refused to accept the government's measures. There was a breakdown in the authority of the central government. Then, as before, Louis XVI gave way. Necker was recalled and within a short time the May edicts were repealed. However, the most important measure was the announcement in August 1788 that the Estates-General would be convoked and would meet on 1 May 1789.

In August 1788 Necker is recalled to direct
the country's finances and this is represented as
a great moment in French history.

The news that the Estates-General were to meet introduced an entirely new
element into the discussion. They would have to be elected, and most Frenchmen over the age of twenty-five would have the right to express an opinion. But
how were they to function? The suggestion that the Estates should deliberate
and vote separately meant that the clergy and the nobility would have a permanent advantage over the Third Estate; if they met together, the more numerous
Third Estate would have the advantage. In the animated discussion which
seems to have gone on throughout the country during 1788 and 1789, there
was a hardening of class attitudes.

The excitement was all the greater because 1788 had been a year when the
harvest had been disastrous. A combination of drought and storm caused a
50 per cent rise in the price of bread in Paris by mid-September 1788. This led
to a decrease of national purchasing power and affected industry. It so happened
that both cattle-farmers and wine-growers were also in particular difficulties,
and when one remembers the ten-year depression which had gone before, then
it is clear that the economic situation was worse than it had been for many
years. The poorer sections of the population were obviously worst hit by the
high cost of bread, but all classes were affected. It was possible, although mis-
taken, to blame the government for what was happening since it had signed
a commercial treaty with England in 1786.

Thus there is a combination of economic and political crisis; there is the
old problem of popular disorder; there is the ancient issue of the powers of the
crown and the need to devise an effective system of government; there is the
question of the unity of the kingdom and the coherence of its society. All these
elements were coming together in 1789.

The clergy and the nobility are shown as being alarmed as they see the Third Estate awakening and removing his chains.

The Estates-General were formally opened on 5 May 1789. The Third Estate insisted, in vain, that the three orders should meet together; on 17 June it therefore declared itself a National Assembly and was joined by some of the clergy, and on 20 June the members of the Assembly swore that they would not be disbanded. As had happened before, the king gave way and on 27 June he accepted that the other orders should join the National Assembly. This then turned to a discussion of constitutional reform and named itself the Constituent Assembly.

But with disturbances continuing in many parts of the country the situation was by no means calm. Rioters demanded that the price of bread be fixed, people seized grain, workers demonstrated because they had not been paid, municipal authorities were often faced with violence. Serious riots had taken place in Paris. In April 1789 the house of a manufacturer, Réveillon, had been attacked because he was reported as advocating a reduction of workers' wages. In the ensuing affray some three hundred people were killed. There were many reports of attacks on excise posts, market-places, châteaux, monasteries, and there were stories of conspiracies and plots. There were rumours that the king's cousin, the duke of Orleans, was in league with the demonstrators; there were accounts of brigands roaming the countryside; it seemed that certain of the forces of order were acting only half-heartedly; it was reported that the king was bringing strong forces of troops into Paris.

The belief that the king would assert himself and bring a halt to all proceedings was confirmed when on 11 July 1789 he dismissed Necker. On 12 July, a Sunday, this news was greeted with indignation. It was widely believed that this action would lead to a rise of prices and to a declaration of bankruptcy. Orators and activists appeared, urging the population to take action; on the night of 12–13 July some fifty customs posts were attacked and set on fire; buildings which were thought to contain foodstuffs were ransacked; those who were electors to the Estates-General attempted to establish a committee and a militia. The Bourse was closed and financiers and bankers thereby seemed to give their approval to the demonstrations, as did the National Assembly at Versailles. On 14 July, in order to gain supplies of arms, the fortress of the Bastille was attacked and taken.

Fall of the Bastille

Armouries were also broken into in Dijon and in Rennes, and although it was the great day of 14 July that has always symbolized the entry of 'the people' on to the stage of French history, the news of the widespread disorder throughout the country made the Assembly realize the urgency of taking action. On 4 and 5 August the end of the feudal system was proclaimed. Sometimes feudal rights, such as tithe, tax exemption, seignorial justice or labour service, were abolished without compensation. Sometimes, money payments were to be made as compensation for seigniorial dues. On 26 August the Declaration of the Rights of

The Declaration of the Rights of Man,
26 August 1789.

On 5 October 1789 about five thousand women, mainly poor but including some who were wealthy, marched from Paris to Versailles. They succeeded in bringing the royal family back to Paris.

Man proclaimed the principle of fundamental human rights. It was true that many of the deputies who voted these measures, out of emotion or fear, afterwards regretted them. Among certain of the clergy and nobility there remained the hope that the king and the army would find a way out of the situation, but in October 1789, there was a curious incident when a shortage of bread, coupled with fear of a royal *coup d'état*, caused a mob of women to march to Versailles. They forced the king and his family to return to Paris. The National Assembly followed and from this time onwards the Revolution became definitive. There could be no going back.

From 1789 to 1792 was the period when the deputies of the Assembly attempted to devise a form of government. The king remained the central figure; he was to govern with an elected Assembly, because sovereignty was inherent in the nation and vested in its representatives. But the nation was divided into those who were 'active' and those who were 'passive'. One was 'active' according to one's wealth, and thereby had rights of eligibility to be a deputy if very wealthy, or to be a voter if less so. Judicial officers and local officials were also to be elected, and the whole country was divided into eighty-three departments (sub-divided into districts, cantons and communes).

This was a period of great reforms. Controls which had inhibited commerce, industry and agriculture were removed; the guilds were abolished; working men's associations were made illegal; some indirect taxes ceased to exist and were replaced by direct taxes which were to be paid by all; internal customs barriers were removed. Sometimes this is called the bourgeois revolution, since the chief beneficiaries were those who were wealthy, and who emerged as the notables in town and country, but a great many nobles were also prominent.

The three orders are represented as co-operating in the creation of the new constitution (1791).

The year 1790 was described as *l'année heureuse*, and it has been asked why it was that the Constitution of 1791 could not provide the basis for a peaceful, successful future. Many thought, by 1791, that the Revolution was over.

There were a number of things which upset these calculations. There was the position of the king. It was a complicated constitution and it required good will to make it work. This was absent both from the king and from his entourage (especially from his politically foolish queen, Marie-Antoinette). Probably, too, one should talk about a slippery slope of revolutionary activity. The explosion of 1788–89 could not easily be channelled into constitutional forms. Political clubs were furthering all sorts of discussion; the influence of many of the Enlightenment thinkers was now quite considerable, although they were quoted by many different groups and for many different purposes.

However, two episodes were particularly important. The one was the decision to seize church land and, regarding it as wealth which belonged to

Marie-Antoinette, painted by Madame Vigée-Lebrun. She is with her daughter Madame Royale, the Dauphin who died in June 1789, and the duc de Normandie (born 1785) who was to be Louis XVII. When this portrait was shown in 1787 an unknown commentator pinned a label to it, saying 'Madame Déficit'.

The money of the Republic,
the assignats.

the nation as a whole, to sell it as a way out of the financial problem. The Civil Constitution of the Clergy (July 1790) set out the consequential governmental responsibility for the Church. The *assignats* were government bonds, based on church land, which were a means of raising the money in anticipation of the sale. The effect of the one was to arouse Catholic opposition to the Revolution and to introduce an ideological division. The effect of the other was to create a form of paper money which was to become harmful to economic life. When the *assignat* became used as currency, and when the number of *assignats* in circulation grew rapidly, then prices rose and as the bad money drove out the good, then the normal process of exchange was hampered.

The other episode was the outbreak of war. The National Assembly had acted in an offhand manner when it had abrogated the rights of the non-French nobility in Alsace and when it seized the Papal possession of Avignon. Emigrating princes and nobles urged foreign rulers to intervene in France. The king hoped to be rescued from a situation which he found increasingly intolerable; politicians, known as the Girondins because many of their leaders came from the Gironde region, hoped that a foreign war would demonstrate the need to take the Revolution a stage further; certain moderates thought that a successful war would consolidate the monarchy and stabilize the Revolution.

It was the French who declared war, in April 1792, against 'the King of Hungary and Bohemia'. This brings a new tempo into the Revolution. When Prussia joined Austria in August it seemed that Paris was threatened. The

A revolutionary committee.

response was a linking of patriotism and revolutionary fervour. The royal palace was invaded on 10 August 1792 and the king became a prisoner; the Constitution of 1791 was abolished and the Convention was elected by universal male suffrage. The enemy was not only the Prussians and Austrians, it was the enemies of the Revolution who were within France itself, the royalists, the aristocrats and the clergy. Rising prices, the shortage of goods and the need to organize the nation in arms meant the end of the liberal experiment. By April 1793 the government was a strong government and was in the hands of committees, especially the Committee of Public Safety and the Committee of General Security. It was not only the economy which had to be regulated: it

The 10th of August 1792 was one of the great revolutionary days. Bertaux's picture (first shown in 1793) shows Swiss guards and national guards killed in the attack on the Tuileries Palace.

The execution of the king, 21 January 1793.

Robespierre.

was society itself which had to be transformed. Just as the king was executed as a measure of public safety (January 1793), as a new calendar was introduced to mark the beginning of a new era, as the Law of the Maximum (September 1793) fixed the prices of basic commodities and wages and as the decrees of Ventôse (March 1794) sought to distribute property to the poor, so there was an attempt to establish a new, rational, useful religion, with the Cult of the Supreme Being. The climax of the Revolution seems to coincide with Robespierre (1758–94) and his dominant position from the spring of 1793 to the summer of 1794. By then the Revolution had defended itself successfully. The Republic was no longer in danger. There was no longer the same need for the excesses of patriotism and revolution. Robespierre was killed, and many who had suffered took their revenge.

From 1795 to 1799 the Directory ruled France, a complicated constitutional arrangement whereby the executive was divided amongst five Directors and a bicameral parliament was chosen by an electorate based on wealth. It was a time of confusion and corruption. At home there was an abortive attempt by Babeuf (1760–97) to raise the working-class of Paris and there were many royalist plots against the bourgeois Republic. Abroad the Directors pursued a policy of conquest and established subservient republics in Holland, Switzer-

The Directory organized great festivals. Here, in 1798, the Directors are seen reviewing art treasures, exotic animals and trophies looted from other countries.

land and Italy. As dissension grew at home and complications were fostered abroad, it was natural enough that the army should come to predominate. In November 1799 it was a general, Napoleon Bonaparte (1769–1821), who had won great renown for his successful campaign in Italy and who had a number of well-placed political friends, who seized power.

There was a considerable contrast between the person of Bonaparte and the Directors who had preceded him. They were mediocre men; Bonaparte was a man of energy and determination, whose abilities as a soldier and administrator have often been regarded as so outstanding as to be unique. But the contrast between him and the Directors should not be exaggerated. Although historians have often written as though the whole history of France after 1799 is to be discerned in the meditations and ambitions of this one man, in reality Napoleon continued many of the policies of his predecessors. It was the manner rather than the principle which differed.

Bonaparte

Thus the centralized administrative system is made more effective by having departments administered by prefects and sub-prefects. The complications of the constitution and of indirect election nullified the effectiveness of universal male suffrage. The long-standing aim of creating a centralized financial system with the private Bank of France controlling the currency, was realized in 1800.

113

The laws were codified. Agreement was signed with Catholic dissidents in western France, and there was an attempt to draw different shades of opinion into a synthesis of government, only avoiding the extremes. Napoleon based his power on his administrative services, on the army, and on the notables. Property remained sacrosanct, including the land taken from the Church and the émigrés; the working-class was at a distinct disadvantage and the machinery of state was geared to the satisfaction of the wealthy. Napoleon was as cynical as any of the politicians of the Directory. Like them he bought friendship and loyalty. Like them he sought to impress by appearance, and by a certain magnificence in his court. Like them he was unable to make any lasting peace in Europe, and after the temporary Peace of Amiens in 1802, there was almost continual war.

Where Napoleon tried to innovate he was less successful. One example is his attempt to solve the religious problem by his Concordat with the Pope (1802), which maintained the pre-Revolutionary tradition that the Gallican Church had some independent rights and which stopped the Directory's experiment of separating Church and State. But the supreme example is the progression of his own power. First Consul out of three in 1799, Consul for life in 1802, Emperor in 1804, the attempt to make his régime the meeting point for all good Frenchmen became a very personal affair. It became an improvisation, since Napoleon could not be everywhere himself and could trust only

Bonaparte visiting the factory of the Sévérin brothers at Rouen in 1802.

The Emperor Napoleon depicted by Ingres (1806)
resembles Charlemagne (*see p. 28*).

A sketch by David shows Napoleon
preparing to crown himself.

Napoleon on the eve of
Austerlitz.

subordinates. The régime became fragile and dependent upon continued military victories. The wars were not popular, and there was discontent at conscription and high taxation, a high rate of desertion from the army and many conspiracies against the Emperor.

Louis XIV had always governed as if he knew that his reign would be long: but Napoleon had no sense of permanence, he was always in a hurry. France could not settle down and Europe could not settle down when Napoleon proposed to make other European countries the market for French goods. The disastrous campaign against Russia (1812), the defeat of Leipzig (1813) and the allied occupation of Paris (1814) were humiliating episodes. The Emperor abdicated and was forced to exchange his imperial crown for the kingship of the tiny island of Elba. Hardly a voice in France was raised on his behalf.

By 1814 it was obvious that the destiny of France was inextricably bound up with the remainder of Europe. It was war which transformed the Revolution in 1792; it was victory which helped to bring to an end the sort of government which seemed typified by Robespierre; it was continuous war which helped to destroy the Directory and it was military defeat which ended the Empire. But war was often an expression of French domestic politics. As has been shown in 1792, there were many different individuals and groups which hoped to be strengthened by war. Napoleon had crushed opposition at home by his victories abroad. French foreign policy had become a reflection of the uncertainties of French government; France, and the French, had acquired the reputa⁄

tion of being restless and dangerous as they involved the rest of Europe in their quest for a régime that would prove permanent and satisfactory. France had been, and was, living dangerously.

All this is illustrated by what followed the abdication of Napoleon. No one accepted his son (by his second marriage, with Marie-Louise of Austria); no one had any idea of what régime could be installed, and the fact that the European allies wanted to restore the Bourbons was sufficient to ensure their return. Louis XVIII (1755–1824), the younger brother of the guillotined Louis XVI – whose son, Louis XVII (1785–95) had died in mysterious circumstances when held prisoner – returned from exile and granted a constitution. In March 1815 Napoleon made his last gamble; he returned to France and, without meeting any resistance, he entered Paris, as Louis XVIII and his court fled to Holland. Napoleon's success can be explained in three ways: by his daring, by a general apathy and indifference, whether to him or to the Bourbons, and, perhaps most important, by a suspicion and a fear that the Bourbon government, with the aristocrats who had flocked back to France, intended to return to the pre-1789 situation, to upset the revolutionary land settlement and restore the feudal rights of the nobility and the Church. But in order to affirm his position, Napoleon had to win military victory. His defeat at Waterloo (1815) caused his final adventure to end with an unhappy exile in the Atlantic ocean, at St Helena.

Louis XVIII returned again and accomplished the feat of dying from natural causes while still ruler of France. His brother, Charles X (1757–1836), was king until he met violent opposition in July 1830, and after three days – *les trois glorieuses* – of fighting in Paris, his son and grandson were passed over and it was the Bourbon cousin, the duke of Orleans (1773–1850) who became Louis-Philippe, king of the French. In 1848 revolution in Paris caused him to abdicate, but his grandson was ignored and the Second Republic was formed in which Napoleon's nephew, Louis Bonaparte (1808–73) was elected President. In 1851 a *coup d'état* and a certain amount of fighting gave him more permanent power and in December 1852 he proclaimed himself Emperor Napoleon III. Like Louis-Philippe, Napoleon lasted for less than eighteen years, but it was defeat by a foreign power, Prussia, that caused the Third Republic to be proclaimed in September 1870. In March 1871 there was a rising in Paris, the Commune. It was patriotic, egalitarian and anti-clerical; it summed up much of the ideals and the ideas of all French revolutionary episodes. It lasted for sixty-two days before it was savagely repressed by the new

Louis XVII died in captivity in June 1795.

A cartoon shows Charles X cracking the nut of the constitution.

Left: Louis-Philippe. A photograph taken in 1845. *Right:* Napoleon III receives plans from Haussmann, the town planner and architect to whom present-day Paris owes so much.

Republic and its President, Thiers. Twenty thousand were killed and many thousands deported.

It is not surprising that France should have gained the reputation of being the revolutionary country *par excellence*, for a revolutionary tradition had grown up. The lesson of history seemed to be that power could be seized; people took to the barricades in the streets of Paris (and occasionally elsewhere) with the self-conscious knowledge that they were acting out a historical role. Other nostalgias were becoming more important. There were those who looked back to the days before 1789 and who had an idyllic picture of a France where the monarch and the various orders of society lived in harmony. Others thought of Napoleon and of how France had achieved unity and order in a great enterprise. And there were others who felt that if only the revolutionary masses had been able to carry through their ideas, then all would have been well.

Naturally, there are particular circumstances which explain the course of French history. Charles X did not have the same adroitness as his brother, he was obstinate and believed that things were as he wished them to be; Louis-Philippe was not respected and was over-pessimistic; Napoleon III was indecisive and, by 1870, very sick. There were accidents. Had Charles X not left Paris when the fighting broke out, communications would have been easier and a compromise could have been reached. Had it not been for a random shooting affray, the revolution of February 1848 might not have got out of hand. The military defeat at Sedan could have been avoided. And it is interesting to see how all the rulers both accepted and rejected their various inheritances. Louis XVIII was king by divine right but he did not wish to upset the administrative and social changes effected by the Revolution. Louis-Philippe was proud of being a descendant of Saint Louis but he was also the king of the barricades. Napoleon III owed his success to his name, but he wanted to have peace and prosperity rather than wars of conquest. There is an ill-adjustment at the heart of nineteenth-century France. Intellectuals and writers tried to explain this as they tried to explain the Revolution and the historical evolution of their country. Some of them, like Madame de Staël (1766–1817), Chateaubriand (1768–1848), Guizot (1787–1874) and Lamartine (1790–1869) were themselves closely involved in the politics of their times.

Guizot. A statesman who was also an educationist, historian and leading French Protestant.

119

Chateaubriand, who is often seen as the archetype of the French romantic.

Daumier's savage cartoon shows the ministerial front bench of 1834.

In one way the problem was an old one. Where in France did sovereignty lie? Did it rest with a monarch or was it elsewhere, somewhere amongst his subjects? The Revolution had complicated the issue. Louis XVIII and Charles X were kings because they were of the royal family. When Napoleon abdicated and the exiled Louis XVIII was told that he was king, he replied that he always had been king. But the Revolution had asserted that there were other rights, and that the people, or at least a section of the people, had rights. Napoleon III was Emperor because he claimed that it was the people's wish, but unlimited power, controlled by one man, supposedly in the name of the people, was not acceptable to everyone.

Between 1815 and 1870 there were various attempts at instituting parliamentary government. Under the monarchies, the right to vote was in the hands of a wealthy minority (in 1830 about 3 per cent of the total population); under the Second Republic there was universal manhood suffrage; under the Second Empire authoritarian government gradually gave way to a form of parliamentary power in which all males had the vote. But there were a number of difficulties.

The novelist Balzac, the actor Lemaître and the poet Théophile Gautier – three great figures of romanticism.

Political parties did not develop as they had in other countries. It seemed as if the complex mosaic of groups and classes that made up French society could not easily fit in to the structure of nineteenth-century political parties. History was making French society more complicated. There were elements which had not changed since before 1789; there were areas which were not touched by industrialization, but in other parts of France, especially under Napoleon III, industrialization occurred rapidly and brought many problems; numbers of Frenchmen found themselves hostile to the Catholic Church, which they suspected of being opposed to progress and socially partisan, while others proclaimed themselves loyal and devoted followers of the Catholic faith and institutions. It was difficult to find an organization which could group together such diversity. The peasantry (in 1870 about 70 per cent of the French population lived in the country) could not be considered as a clear social or political class. The industrial workers, confined to a few towns, could only make an impact by occasional, unsuccessful, insurrections (Lyons 1831 and 1834, Paris 1848).

Throughout the years 1815 to 1870–71 France retained the same centralized administrative machinery. It was argued that the parliamentary system of government could not exist side by side with such an administrative system, since every government had too much power and patronage. It could be argued, too, that such a system increased the chances of revolutionary activity, since Paris, at the centre of the administration, and growing in wealth and population far more than any other town in France, was always at the mercy of revolutionary activity. Perhaps, too, the uninterrupted social power of the wealthy bourgeoisie, which allied itself with the power of the official class, also encouraged revolutionary activity. Such a power, it was thought, could not be modified; it could only be broken. Such a system could not be reformed; it could only be replaced.

The Quai du Louvre, painted by Monet (1866–67).

Perhaps, too, this attitude was not confined to politics. It extended to culture, and France became the centre of the experimental and the innovatory in art and literature.

By 1870 the Second Empire's future was uncertain. Napoleon III resolved to save it by his declaration of war against Germany, but his defeat, and capture, meant that he had played his last card. In Paris the Republic was proclaimed (4 September 1870); once again revolution and patriotism were allied. Paris, which suffered a long and cruel siege by the Germans, became the symbol of patriotism. But even this could not unite the remainder of France. Those who wanted peace, and who were prepared to cede Alsace and Lorraine to the Germans, became most influential. When peace was signed, it was as if the people of Paris were isolated in France. With the Commune they emphasized these differences still further as they claimed their revolutionary heritage and attacked the Church and the bourgeoisie. The Commune showed that revolutionary France fought against its enemies in Europe, and that within revolutionary France, Frenchman fought against Frenchman.

The Third Republic was born in defeat and for many years it lived in uncertainty. Elections had been held in February 1871 and a majority had been returned which was conservative and monarchist. But it had been elected because the Right, rather than the Left, was in favour of making peace, and once the peace terms had been approved and the Commune suppressed, then the divisions amongst the royalists rendered them largely ineffective as a political force; they were not agreed on who should be their king, whether it should be the comte de Chambord, grandson of Charles X, or the comte de Paris, grandson of Louis-Philippe, and there were still those who retained some loyalty to the Bona-partists. Nor was there any agreement as to the constitution which would

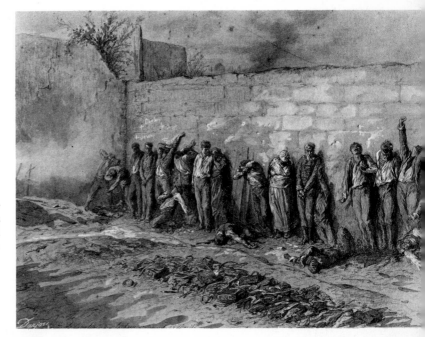

Le mur des Fédérés. In the Père-Lachaise cemetery the supporters of the Commune are executed (28 May 1871).

Adolphe Thiers, having been a
minister of Louis-Philippe and
an opponent of Napoleon III,
became the real founder of the
Third Republic. Under his
direction the Republic was
essentially conservative.

Destruction in a Paris street
during the Commune.

surround the monarch. In this uncertainty Thiers (1797–1877), who was President of the Republic until 1873, and Gambetta (1838–82) urged the existence of a Republic which would be moderate and conservative. On the other hand, Marshal de MacMahon (1808–93), who succeeded Thiers at the Presidency, together with the leaders of the Catholic Church, hoped to bring about a reconciliation between the two dynastic families and in the meantime to re-establish a France of moral values and virtues. It was decided to construct a great basilica in Montmartre in expiation for the insurrection of the Commune. The shock of defeat and of civil war had obviously encouraged those forces that believed that France had taken a wrong turning in 1789. Although the more Radical republicanism had suffered in the repression of the Commune, it still existed and could emerge, particularly in Paris, as an anti-clerical and social force.

As is well-known, the royalist cause was completely compromised by the comte de Chambord's refusal to accept the three-coloured flag of France. In 1789, when the blue and red colours of Paris had been joined to the white of the Bourbon monarchy, this had become the patriotic and revolutionary symbol of France. The comte de Chambord insisted that he would only have

Utrillo's painting of a street in Montmartre, showing the Basilica of the Sacré-Cœur.

Caricature of
Marshal MacMahon.

the white of the Bourbons, but by this time the Republic had had the immense advantage of having existed. The indemnity which the Germans had exacted had been paid and all German occupying troops evacuated; there was general prosperity and *la république bourgeoise* was not unattractive to many. A revival of Bonapartism after Napoleon III's death in 1873 (his son was then aged seventeen) was seen as alarming and it appeared prudent to organize a more definitive constitution before the situation changed. Thus, in February 1875, a conservative Republican, Wallon, rallied a Republican-Orleanist majority in the Assembly. His amendment, which was accepted by one vote, officially established the Presidency of the Republic. The constitutional laws were then voted by substantial majorities.

Republic or Monarchy? The elections of 1876 produced a clear Republican majority in the Assembly. Soon it was at odds, particularly over religious matters, with the President, MacMahon. The President forced a monarchist, Bonapartist and clerical government to face the Assembly, and some time after it had failed to win a vote of confidence on 16 May 1877, he dissolved the Assembly. The elections, which were not held until October, were fought most fiercely. On the one hand MacMahon, who was supported by the Catholics, attempted to manipulate the elections by administrative pressure. There could still be a chance to restore the monarchy. On the other hand, the Republicans, under Gambetta, claimed to be fighting for a parliamentary system, against royalism, clericalism and reaction. The result was that the Republicans were returned with a reduced majority. It was not long before MacMahon resigned and it could be said that the Third Republic had definitively established itself.

In many ways, this Republic did not appear to be strong. The political confusions which had characterized the period following defeat at Sedan were still apparent after 1875. It appeared impossible for a government to be formed which had any hope of lasting more than a short time. Ministerial instability became the most obvious characteristic of the régime, and if the average length of a government was a matter of some nine months, there were many governments who were destined to be in office for much shorter periods. The instability of governments was linked to the political spectrum. There were always at least five major political groups, though they could confuse their identity beneath a variety of party labels. Thus there was invariably a group corresponding to the extreme right and a group corresponding to the extreme left; a group which can best be described as right centre and a group which was left centre; finally, there were usually groups which held some position in the centre. Not only were the frontiers between these groups fluid and variable; the politicians were also opportunist and had all the dexterity and subtlety which were necessary to play the political game. The outstanding fact is that no one political party ever won an over-all majority in the Chamber of Deputies, and if one talks, for example, of the Republic majorities of 1876 and 1877, this is to refer

Thiers receives an ovation in the Chamber of Deputies in 1877.

only to the one issue, that of Republic or monarchy. Within the Republicans were many different ideals and organizations, and if the social diversity of France and the historical complexity of the French past were the main causes of this situation, there were other reasons which explain this evolution.

The problem of where sovereignty lay took on a new aspect. The experience of Bonapartism and the episode of President de MacMahon confirmed those who believed in the danger of strong government. From then onwards the Presidency of the Republic was in the hands of men whose ambitions were limited and who saw their functions as largely ceremonial. Throughout the existence of the Third Republic no President imitated MacMahon and dissolved the Chamber, but this was his undoubted constitutional right. The 1875 laws had given considerable powers to the President. He was head of the executive, presided over cabinet meetings and was elected for seven years by an absolute majority of the two houses of Parliament meeting together (the Senate and the Chamber of Deputies). Since he did not effectively use these powers, it has to be asked who inherited them in his place. It was hardly the Prime Minister (or Président du Conseil, as he should be called). He, and his ministers, could control the President both constitutionally (since every act of the President had to be countersigned by a minister) and through influence, but the Prime Minister was dependent upon Parliament and did not have the right to order a dissolution. Hence there was a certain diffusion of power, in which it was the divided, and often unruly, Chamber of Deputies which seemed to have the last word.

The voting system which was adopted in 1875 was intended to increase the prestige of the individual deputy. Electoral constituencies elected a single member, but unless a candidate received the absolute majority of the votes cast on the first ballot, there was a second ballot where a relative majority only was required. Such a system (which was occasionally modified) encouraged local variations in politics and undoubtedly contributed to the multiplicity of parties and to their fragmentation.

Behind the details of political controversy there were major areas of conflict. The one was the religious issue. The Catholic Church had associated itself with the restoration of the monarchy and although there were many exceptions among Catholics themselves, the institutions of the Catholic Church appeared as enemies of the Republic. It was thus necessary to create a Republican ideal, and forge a Republican unity, which was anti-clerical. This was all the more natural since Pius IX, by his condemnation of the errors of liberalism,

The Religious Question

rationalism and socialism, and by his doctrine of Papal Infallibility had placed the Church in an exposed position. Laws were passed against unauthorized religious associations and in 1882 primary education was made free, secular and compulsory; civil marriage was also made compulsory; the state became ostentatiously lay in all its public ceremonial.

There was also the social question. By 1914 there were some six million industrial workers in France, and although the majority of them were employed in small enterprises, there were areas, such as the mining and metallurgical industries, where concentration was considerable.

Many observers were struck, not so much by the poverty and the bad living conditions of this section of the community, as by their isolation. A whole world seemed to separate them from other Frenchmen. This isolation was apparent in the way in which trade-union activity (trade unions became legal again in 1884 and the General Confederation of Labour was founded in 1895) was independent from the political organization of the Socialists (who were unified in 1905). The Socialists took part in the great game of politics. The working-class, often convinced that governments had forgotten them or were directly hostile to their interests, remained loyal to a tradition of the Revolution, going back to Babeuf: they would one day seize power. Naturally, as always in France, this working-class was soon diversified, and within the CGT itself, the insurrectionists were counterbalanced by moderates. But the problem of the integration of the working-class remained. Like the cultural problem of relations between Catholics and anti-clericals it was illustrated in two of the great crises which shook the régime.

Between 1886 and 1889 the political scene was largely dominated by General Boulanger (1837–91), who had served as minister for war. The attractions of this handsome, dashing soldier were augmented by the revelation of corruption in the entourage of Grévy (1807–91), President of the Republic. Some supporters of 'Boulangisme' thought that a constitutional reform was needed, so that France could have a strong rather than a weak government. This was all the more necessary since France was conscious of her weakness in Europe, especially *vis-à-vis* a united and powerful Germany. The idea of a war of revenge against Germany might not have been taken seriously by responsible soldiers, but it was a cry which was popular, and there could have been few Frenchmen who had resigned themselves to the loss of Alsace and Lorraine. Boulanger, as a person and as an ideal, corresponded to a national ideal. He rallied monarchists and workers, while insisting that he was Republican. The idea was that Boulanger

The leader of the revolution that did not take place. General Boulanger wears his spurs.

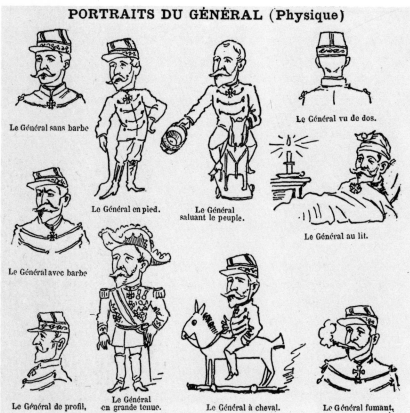

Cartoons of Boulanger.

could unite the different attitudes and aspirations of the French in a great national enterprise which was in contrast to the petty preoccupations of the opportunists. That the Boulanger 'revolution' was a failure, and ended with the flight of the General and with his eventual suicide, was in part the fault of the General himself. He was indecisive and uncertain, probably incapable of playing the role that he had assigned himself. But his defeat was also due to the skill with which the Republican parties organized their riposte.

It was important for 'the Dreyfus affair' that it came after this unsuccessful revolution, and also after a particularly notorious scandal when a great many deputies had been bribed by financiers and had accepted not to raise embarrassing questions about the progress of the Panama Canal. The arrest and condemnation of Captain Dreyfus (1859–1935) on a charge of spying might otherwise have appeared as unimportant. But by 1894, the date of Dreyfus' arrest, there were many exposed nerves in France. It soon seemed apparent to many Frenchmen that Dreyfus had been unjustly condemned and that the army and the government were engaged in a plot which was clerical, militarist and anti-Semite (Dreyfus, like many of the financiers in the Panama scandal, was Jewish). To others it seemed equally certain that there was a conspiracy among foreigners, intellectuals and egocentric politicians, to endanger the security of the state and to weaken the morale of the army. The articulate passions of the *affaire* have probably magnified its importance. It was not until 1899 that a compromise

The Dreyfus Case

Captain Dreyfus, during his retrial at Rennes, walks between guards who turn their backs on him.

Au jour prochain, on rendra ses galons à
Dreyfus et la France glorieuse réparera noble-
ment l'injustice faite à un de ses soldats les
plus dévoués.

A contemporary drawing shows France presiding over the rehabilitation of Dreyfus.

was found whereby Dreyfus was pardoned, although still theoretically guilty, and it was not until 1906 that he was declared innocent. The *affaire* not only illuminated the divisions existing within France, but also contributed to them. From this time onwards there were many who could not accept the nationalism of the Right, however desirable or logical it might have been, because the Right wanted to keep Dreyfus in prison. The separation between Church and State (1905) was a direct consequence of the affair.

Yet the Republic continued; in fact it could be said that after both crises it emerged stronger than before. The Boulanger affair made it less likely that anyone, outside the extremists, would seek to change the constitution. The Dreyfus affair had its attempted *coup d'état* but it had been ludicrous rather than dangerous. Ernest Constans (1833–1913) had emerged as a Republican leader who had organized the defeat of Boulangism; the Waldeck-Rousseau (1846–1904) government, which was called into being in order to liquidate the Dreyfus affair, was one of the most widely based and long lived (1898–1902) of the Third Republic. The 'defence of the Republic', on both occasions, was a mechanism whereby the working-class could associate itself enthusiastically with the institutions and men of the bourgeoisie.

It is easy to exaggerate the extent of instability. Although governments came and went, the political personnel was limited, and a change of ministry could be little more than a re-shuffle. The administrative system remained a great unifying force, but the essence of the strength of the Third Republic lay in its social structure.

The French population, since about 1846, had been growing more slowly than the populations of other countries. The days of the eighteenth century when France had the largest population in Europe (Russia excepted) were far away. In 1876 the population was about 37 million; by the census of 1911 this had become 39 million. The birth-rate was low and the death-rate (particularly of infantile mortality) was high. This relative stagnation is probably explicable in terms of mentality, a lack of self-confidence in the light of past famines, disturbances, crises and invasions. It must also be explicable in terms of particular factors such as the growth of Paris and the difficulty of organizing adequate medical services in a large rural country, or the continuation of revolutionary legislation whereby property had to be divided equally among children rather than inherited by the eldest son. But the effect of such a slow population growth was clear enough. There was little pressure from new generations. Movements from the countryside to the towns were limited, and emigration from France was small.

It could also be that the slow population growth helps to explain the relatively slow industrialization of the country, since demand remained stable. We should also take into account some inconvenience in the supply and location of raw materials, a shortage of speculative capital and a preference for investment in land or in government bonds, and a general lack of entrepreneurial spirit. The result was that while England, Germany and Belgium had, by 1914, become overwhelmingly industrial countries, in France 41 per cent of the active population was still in agriculture. Just under a half of those engaged in commerce and industry were self-employed, thereby demonstrating the predominance of the small, artisanal, often family, firm.

Climbing up the Eiffel tower was rewarded with a souvenir medal.

Marcel Proust.

Claude Debussy.

Two poets together: Paul Verlaine and Charles Rimbaud.

Jacques-Emile Blanche painted André Gide and his friends, sitting in a mock native café in the Tunisian quarter of the Universal Exposition (1900).

Captain Marchand and a small detachment of French troops nearly precipitated an Anglo-French war when they raised the tricolor over Fashoda on the Nile in 1898. The picture shows Marchand and his men before they were recalled.

It was this which was the strength of the Republic. If it was difficult to bring such a mosaic of traditions and conditions into a monolithic political structure, the loose organization of government seemed usually to afford a large measure of satisfaction. Those who interpret history in terms of class relationships can point to a salaried smaller bourgeoisie which shared political power with the upper bourgeoisie. Once the peasantry had accepted the Republic and had been won over to supporting Republican parties, then *une république bourgeoise* was an institution which presented the appearance rather than the reality of disunity. The Third Republic corresponded to the possessive individualism of most of the country. Patriotism was another source of unity. It was true that colonialism was never popular. The conquests of the Third Republic, in Tunisia, Indo-China, Madagascar and large areas of Africa, were often the work of individuals or of particular interest groups. Some Frenchmen thought that the acquisition of colonies was a distraction from the main issue, which was France's relations with Germany. At the time of the Dreyfus affair, questions of foreign policy were, for some, overshadowed by anti-militarism and, later, by the ideals of international socialism. But as the twentieth century progressed, as the alliance system hardened, then a greater patriotism enclosed all Frenchmen. When war broke out in 1914 it was greeted with enthusiasm and the cause of national defence created unity, *l'union sacrée*.

DIGNITY AND IMPUDENCE.

British indignation over Fashoda, expressed in a political cartoon.

137

CRÉDIT COMMERCIAL DE FRANCE

4ème Emprunt de la Défense Nationale - 1918

SOUSCRIVEZ POUR LA VICTOIRE
ET POUR LE TRIOMPHE DE LA LIBERTÉ

A poster urges the French to invest in the Allied cause. France presides over an Italian, a French and a British soldier, whilst the Americans are seen arriving in endless numbers.

French infantry on the march, 1914.

The war of 1914 to 1918 was to prove the solidarity of the Third Republic and disprove those who believed that France was decadent. It justified those who had claimed that a state system of education would create a sentiment of unity. It justified the belief that Frenchmen could forget all that divided them when they were forced to remember all that united them as a nation. With Russia and Britain as allies, France appeared as a strong country.

The war began badly for the French. The Germans advanced through Belgium and overcame resistance at various places. By the beginning of September, German troops were crossing the Marne, the French government took the precaution of installing itself in Bordeaux and Paris prepared to be attacked. The French commander, Joffre, re-grouped his forces in the Paris region, and taking advantage of German mistakes, launched his counter-offensive. On 9 September the Germans started to withdraw from the Marne and established themselves on the Aisne, on a line running roughly from Verdun to Noyon, which was then extended, running northwards through Arras and Ypres to the sea.

By the end of 1914 the French had lost 380,000 men killed, and 600,000 wounded, prisoners or missing. In particular a remarkably high rate of infantry officers had been killed or wounded during the French offensives. Exhausted, both sides began digging in and the long agony of trench warfare began. It became impossible to break the lines, although this remained a hope for nearly four years.

Thus the war became a long war. The enthusiasm of 1914 had been in the expectation of a short war, and also in expectation of victory. Although the

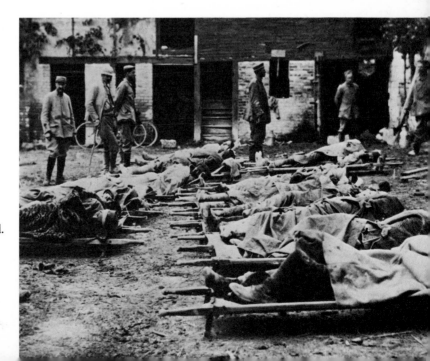

French wounded.

Foch signs the armistice, 11 November 1918.

battle of the Marne had been a defeat for the Germans, in so far as they had had
to abandon their plans, it could hardly be called a great victory for the French.
German troops occupied about one-tenth of French territory. Neither the spring
nor the autumn offensives of 1915 could dislodge them. The battle of Verdun
in 1916 was a French victory in so far as the Germans abandoned their attacks,
but with French casualties higher than German, it could hardly be called a
victory. In 1917 General Nivelle, who had replaced Joffre as commander-in-
chief, ordered a new offensive; but the French infantry were slaughtered as they
advanced into artillery and machine-gun fire. It is hardly surprising that
numbers of French troops felt that they could no longer carry on, and there was
a wave of mutinies. Pétain (1856–1951), the hero of Verdun and a general
reputed to be careful of men's lives in all his plans, replaced Nivelle. In 1918
the allies fell back as the Germans attacked strongly and reached the Marne.
In April Foch (1851–1929) had been made inter-allied commander, and from
mid-July he began to counter-attack. French, British and American troops

pushed the Germans back. Although there was never any decisive break-through, by October the Germans were exhausted and as their allies deserted them, requested the armistice that came on 11 November.

Thus France had won the war. There had been domestic crises as well as military, as with a series of strikes in 1917, and the Socialists' resignation from the government when the government would not allow them to attend the International Socialist conference at Stockholm. There had been the economic problems, too, of organizing supplies when so much of the nation's coal, iron ore and wheat were in German hands. There was the problem of relations between Parliament and the government, and through the government, relations with the generals. But all these problems were eased when the President of the Republic, Raymond Poincaré (1860–1934), appointed a man whom he greatly disliked, Georges Clemenceau (1841–1929), as Prime Minister in November 1917. Clemenceau seemed to embody the old revolutionary virtues. His patriotism made him acceptable to the right. His anti-clericalism and republic-anism made him acceptable to the left. With this remarkable old man striking the imagination of soldiers and civilians alike, there was no danger of a political crisis which could have led France into a military dictatorship or socialism. Clemenceau symbolized the nation's will for victory: but he also symbolized the Republic.

Clemenceau with his allies in 1918.

The signing of the peace treaty in the Hall of Mirrors, Versailles, 1919.

There were many effects of the war in France, but three major considerations were to dominate French life in the 1920's and 1930's. The first was that the demographic effect of four years of fighting in a country which already had an ageing population was catastrophic. More than 1,300,000 Frenchmen were killed; more than 1,100,000 were permanently invalided; there had been an increase in civilian deaths; the birth-rate had been abnormally low. Counting deaths, and counting the births which did not take place, it has been calculated that the war resulted in a haemorrhage of some 3,000,000. Strategically, economically and psychologically this was an unparalleled disaster.

The second major consideration involved France's economy. Whether because the bourgeoisie had preferred to give its sons rather than give up its gold, or whether because a harsh taxation policy would have been unbearable

In the station at Verdun, 1920: Monsieur Maginot, the founder of the famous defence system, Raymond Poincaré, Monsieur Lefevre (then Minister for War) and Marshal Pétain.

in a country undergoing the agonies of 1914–18, the war had been financed by a policy of expensive loans. The reconstruction of the devastated areas, carried out with great efficiency, was also financed by loans. Therefore by the 1920's the government debt was considerable, and the government was operating by inflation. The legend persisted that it was the Germans who would pay and that massive payments of reparation would somehow solve all of France's problems. But by 1924 it was clear that this would not happen. In the elections of that year a left-wing coalition was victorious, and Edouard Herriot (1872–1957), a Radical, became Prime Minister. The crisis was underlined in a number of ways. There was a loss of confidence in the franc. Its value on the international money market declined rapidly. There was a flight of capital from France. Herriot was ill at ease on financial matters, and typical of the majority of French statesmen in not understanding what was happening. It was clear that there would have to be some redistribution of taxation, but while their Socialist allies spoke of a capital levy and a reduction in the interest rates of government bonds, the Radicals were conscious of the fact that many of their clientèle were themselves small-scale investors and capital-holders. Thus the Radicals made verbal gestures in the direction of a capital levy and found themselves at odds with the banking interests. The result was the defeat of the government and a series of cabinet crises, punctuated by the continued fall of the franc. In July 1926 Poincaré became Prime Minister for the fourth time. By increasing taxes, though not altering the distribution of taxation, by reducing government expenditure and by restoring confidence, he was able to re-establish the value of the franc in 1928.

The effect of all this was to create a kind of neurosis about the franc. When the world depression drove other countries to go off the gold standard and to

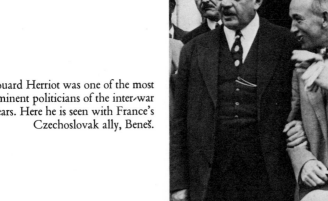

Edouard Herriot was one of the most prominent politicians of the inter-war years. Here he is seen with France's Czechoslovak ally, Beneš.

devalue their currencies, up to 1936 the French clung doggedly to the Poincaré franc. The stability of the currency seemed more important than the level of economic activity. The large number of family firms or family-run farms ought to have cushioned France against the worst effects of the slump, but in fact industrial production and foreign exports all fell and unemployment increased. Edouard Herriot was never to forget his experience of 1925 and was always to believe in the existence of important financial interests, *le mur d'argent*, which could intervene politically. Many other Frenchmen also believed in this and thought that France was in danger of falling into the hands of selfish bankers and financiers.

The third major consideration which emerged from the war was the importance of France's foreign relations. France had won the war but it had been necessary to have Russia, Britain, Italy and the United States as allies. The problem of French security was to dominate the policies of all French statesmen, and France was never able to get satisfaction from her allies. France wanted Germany to be dismembered, but this was rejected. France was promised an alliance system, but it was dropped. Clauses in the Versailles treaty were meant to ensure a long period of keeping Germany down, and in 1923 the French government occupied the Ruhr in an attempt to enforce the treaty to the full. But gradually the Versailles treaty became a dead letter. Edouard Herriot tried to get security by making the League responsible for some international force, but this scheme (the Protocol) failed. Aristide Briand (1862–1932) helped to initiate the policy of treaty agreement in which Germany was included. The idea of France having allies in eastern Europe, notably Poland and Czechoslovakia, was also tried. But by the time the Nazis came to power in Germany and started on a rearmament programme, France still had no effective system. Each French government was forced to make a considerable effort to maintain French military strength. A massive line of defence, the Maginot Line, was started in 1930. But, though every Frenchman knew that against Germany France had to have allies, it was difficult to find them. In terms of international diplomacy France had become a dependent power.

It is hardly surprising that in the light of these major difficulties, there was a considerable strain on the political system. The average length of a government in the period between 1920 and 1940 was even less than that before 1914, being about seven months. The inadequacy of the political system was most obvious during the 1930's. Poincaré, who had largely dominated the 1920's with his two long administrations of 1922–24 (when the Ruhr was occupied) and 1926–29 (that

Aristide Briand, who dominated French foreign policy in the 1920's, leaving the British Foreign Office in 1925, after calling on his friend Austen Chamberlain.

The ruins of a barricade in the Boulevard Sébastopol, during the 1934 riots.

of the stabilization of the franc) retired in July 1929. A new generation of politicians was to appear. It was as if the Third Republic was losing something of its solidarity when Clemenceau died in 1929, Briand in 1932, Poincaré in 1934.

The year 1934 was one of dramatic crisis. A minor affair concerning a crooked financier, Stavisky, became important when it was known that he had had friends in high places. The government had to resign and when Edouard Daladier (1884–1970) became Prime Minister, his dismissal of the Paris police chief caused a number of right-wing groups and ex-servicemen's leagues to demonstrate. A large-scale confrontation on 6 February led to at least fourteen people being killed, and in the next few days a further thirteen were killed, while more than 2,000 were injured. The government resigned and was replaced by a ministry which included Pétain. It was suggested that the French right wing had almost seized power, that the presence of Marshal Pétain in the government meant that there was going to be a move towards authoritarianism, and there were rumours about military involvement.

The year 1936 also saw its drama and crisis. The Communists and Socialists (who had separated in 1920) joined with the Radicals in winning an election victory. With the Socialists as the largest party in the Assembly it was clear that their leader Léon Blum (1872–1950) would become Prime Minister. Before he took office an unprecedented wave of strikes took place and it was in an atmosphere of excited enthusiasm that the Popular Front government took power, and inaugurated its reforms. But by June 1937 the Blum government had resigned. There was bitter disappointment over the realization that the Blum government had, after all, been like any other government. There was bitterness, too, between the different groups that had made up the coalition,

Léon Blum leaves his house for the Chamber of Deputies on the eve of becoming Prime Minister in 1936.

particularly over the attitude which had been adopted towards the Spanish Civil War. Blum had devalued the franc, and while for many this was in itself a betrayal, there were others who thought his action had come too late. He had introduced the forty-hour week and holidays with pay; many saw this as striking at France's productive capacity. The bourgeoisie were alarmed, the workers disillusioned. It was a social revolution with all the disadvantages.

It should not be thought that the France which went to war with Germany in 1939 was deeply pessimistic about the outcome. The Prime Minister was Daladier, who had served in Blum's Popular Front government and who had been Minister for Defence since 1936. It was widely believed that the French army was the finest in the world and that the commander-in-chief, General Gamelin, had evolved an effective method of defensive warfare. There was a general expectation that with British and Commonwealth economic power, the allies were far stronger than the Germans. After the German-Soviet pact, there was wide agreement in France that it was the Communists who were the enemies inside the French state.

The rapid disintegration of the French army, when the Germans took the offensive by invading Holland and Belgium on 10 May 1940, came therefore as an astonishing surprise. Within a month the French war machine had been destroyed and a week later a French government was asking for an armistice.

The German success can be described in three phases. While the invasion of Holland and Belgium drew the allies into those countries, the German Panzer divisions crossed the Ardennes and succeeded in crossing the Meuse. The Germans then struck westward, dividing the allies into two and forcing the evacuation of allied forces from Dunkirk. Finally, between the 7th and 9th of June the Germans attacked the French line established from Abbeville *Fall of France* to the Maginot Line and succeeded in breaking it. When Italy declared war on 10 June the disaster was complete.

Many reasons have been given for French failure. At the time it was said that the French army was ill-equipped, that its officers had betrayed it, that France had been filled with enemy agents. More politically it was alleged that the French generals and bourgeoisie preferred to have Hitler in France than another government led by Léon Blum. It was claimed that the British had given little assistance; that the panic of the civilian population, running away from areas which were thought dangerous, had hampered military operations; that many politicians were only too happy to end the war which they feared could only lead to a killing of Frenchmen on the 1914 scale.

Changing guard in the Maginot Line, 1940.

British and French prisoners at Dunkirk, 1940.

Civilians flee before the German advance in 1940.

Nowadays one tends to emphasize points of detail: the French command did not know how to make use of its resources, communications were badly organized, there was a degree of over-planning, no one was capable of launching a vigorous counter-attack, French troops broke when dive-bombed. But one also emphasizes a very general point. In the summer of 1940, a gigantic effort was needed if the French were to survive. Paul Reynaud, who had succeeded Daladier as Prime Minister, seemed disposed to organize that effort. But as the confusion grew, the refusal to make the effort also grew. Reynaud himself gave up and was succeeded by Pétain. It was as if no one in France could face another war like that of 1914–18.

One thing is clear. From 1940 French history has three aspects. Marshal Pétain abolished the Republic and headed the French state, with its capital at Vichy, while the Germans occupied Paris and much of French territory. General de Gaulle (1890–1970), who had held a junior post in Reynaud's government, went to London and organized Free France. Eventually a resistance movement developed within both occupied and unoccupied France. Vichy, Gaullism and the Resistance were agreed on one principle: it was necessary for France to break away from the traditions of the Third Republic.

The Fourteenth of July, 1940. General de Gaulle reviews the Free French forces in London.

Chapter Seven

It had often been suggested that the period of French revolutions had come to
an end. The unsuccessful rising of the Commune in 1871 had been a classical
example of the revolution which did not come off; Boulangism and the riots of
6 February 1934 (when crowds had failed to break into the National Assembly)
had been other, paler, examples. It was always admitted that if for some reason
the government were to be rendered ineffective, then there would be an opportunity for revolution. This was the situation in the summer of 1940. But it was
the forces of 'counter-revolution' which were the first to realize the political
implications of the military defeat. The air became heavy with assaults on the
revolutionary, republican tradition. It was allegedly the lay, parliamentary,
individualistic and politics-ridden state which was responsible for the defeat.
Accordingly a series of constitutional changes abolished the Presidency and
the Parliament. Marshal Pétain became Chief of the French State with the
power to name his successor. The revolutionary motto of *liberté, égalité, fraternité*
was replaced by *famille, patrie, travail.* The emphasis was on the religious and
moral values; large families were encouraged, youth was organized in patriotic
groupings, capitalists and workers were supposed to work together in corporate
institutions; the peasant landowner was considered to be the keystone of the
régime; non-French elements, such as Jews, were attacked and persecuted;
Socialists and Communists were regarded as the enemies of France.

    This then was the National Revolution. But whereas there were some theorists
who were entirely devoted to this ideal, there were many other sides to Vichy.
Its whole existence was dominated by the German occupation of the northern
three-fifths of France and by relations between Germany and the unoccupied
zone. Some individual Frenchmen believed in whole-hearted collaboration

with the Germans and in the role which France would play in Hitler's new Europe. But a more considerable body of opinion believed neither in this collaboration, nor in the principles of the National Revolution. They believed in bargaining with the Germans, in defending French interests in every possible way. There was a crisis, but France had the advantage of having been granted a semi-independent government, and the essential task was to use the opportunities which this afforded. The leader of this side was Pierre Laval (1883–1945).

Pétain belonged to all sides in Vichy. He was himself an opportunist and his fundamental belief was that he was saving France from the fate of Poland. He thought that his military reputation could impress Hitler, and that he could defend the interests of the French people and the French empire. He also had the idea that France should undergo the experience of a new form of government; in this, he might have been influenced by his experience of the Franco régime in Spain, where he had for a time served as French ambassador. There might well have been a touch of senility about him, since he was eighty-three when he became Chief of State. But he was pleased by the unexpected windfall of coming to power and showed great political skill in avoiding any dominant influence

The leaders of the Vichy government (*opposite*). To the left of the aged Marshal Pétain stand Admiral Darlan and Pierre Laval; behind them, a civilian between two generals, is Darquier de Pellepoix, commissioner for Jewish affairs, and behind Laval is General Noguès, Resident-General in Morocco. *Right:* nearing the end of his time – Pétain is cheered by the crowd in Paris, May 1944.

and in keeping his options open. He made secret advances to many different organizations, both French and foreign.

The real crisis of the Vichy régime occurred in November 1942. It was then that British and American forces invaded North Africa and the Germans occupied the whole of France. For many it seemed that Vichy should now negotiate with the Americans and that because North Africa (Morocco, Algeria, Tunisia) was under French rule, France had a particular role to play in the development of the war. The events of 1942 greatly encouraged the Resistance movements within France.

In its earliest days, from 1940 onwards, the Resistance had been an affair of individuals and small groups. People were in the Resistance because they were patriots, or adventurers, or pursued by the authorities. Many Communists were already in hiding before the accession of Pétain, since they had been attacked by Daladier's government. It seems probable that some of them were active in resistance from the beginning. But only after the German invasion of Russia in 1941 was their contribution to the Resistance massive. Then the Resistance became ideological. The work of the Resistance was not only military, preparing for the overthrow of the Germans and their collaborators,

Resistance

151

A rare picture of the Resistance in action – a train lies derailed and 800 German prisoners are in French hands.

but also political. A great deal of energy was devoted to the production of clandestine literature; drawing their inspiration frequently from the Popular Front, they attributed French defeat to reactionary, bourgeois elements; they looked forward to a new régime in which the people would hold power.

The Resistance movement was extremely varied, but all elements were looking for help from outside France. This came from the Free French forces established in London under the leadership of General de Gaulle. The Gaullist movement was far more of a unity than either Vichy or the Resistance movements, since it was dominated by a young and relatively unknown junior general, who had had a brief experience of government under Reynaud. He had the reputation of having understood the sort of war which was going to develop; intensely patriotic, he went out of his way to demonstrate that he was independent both of the British and of the Americans; he encouraged the idea that with the liberation there would be a great meting-out of justice and that the ordinary

French people, who had been betrayed by their leaders, were allied together in a unity personified by him, General de Gaulle.

In 1942 de Gaulle's representative, Jean Moulin, was parachuted into France. Although he was later tortured and killed by the Germans, he laid the foundations for the coming together of the resistance movements. The National Council of the Resistance was formed in 1943 and was allied with de Gaulle. This proved one of the great sources of Gaullist strength.

On 6 June 1944 the allies invaded Normandy. The Americans and the British hoped to eliminate de Gaulle, whom they had found too difficult and who they suspected was both dictatorial and influenced by the Communists. But those areas of France which were able to express themselves showed that they were Gaullist; wherever de Gaulle went he was acclaimed. The rising of

D-Day – 6 June 1944. The Normandy beaches swarm with Allied landing craft, tanks and soldiers – and the Free French are among them.

On 25 August 1944 came the great day when de Gaulle returned to Paris. He marched in triumph down the Champs Elysées and all Paris rose to him.

the Resistance movement in Paris struck the imagination of everyone and Gaullist forces under General Leclerc were sent to Paris. On 25 August 1944 Paris was liberated; the next day de Gaulle strode in triumph down the Champs Elysées.

Liberation The liberation of Paris did not bring about the end of the war in France and it was not until the spring of 1945 that all areas were freed. The liberation was not a moment of universal rejoicing, since it was also the time of the *épuration*, when those who had collaborated with the Germans were purged. Many were killed by partisans during and after the liberation, and there were some summary executions, as well as cases of political and private vengeance. A number of Vichy leaders were brought to trial, including Laval (who was executed) and Pétain (who was given life imprisonment). Sometimes it was pointed out

In the aftermath of liberation, the *épuration*. Laval (*left*), wildly gesticulating in self-vindication, was condemned to death. Pétain, dignified in defeat, received a life sentence.

that the record of the judge or of the public prosecutor in the trial was no better than that of the accused. It was therefore a time of great bitterness. It was also a time of hardship. Food was short, especially in the towns, and the rationing system was badly organized; industrial production was low, the transport system had broken down, many ports were not functioning; in Normandy about half a million people were homeless or living in damaged houses.

Politically there was more than a hint of anarchy, since Resistance leaders ruled over large parts of the country. Government had to be an improvisation, an attempt to get things going again and to restore the authority of the state.

But it was a moment of hope and enthusiasm. The role of the Resistance and the fact that de Gaulle had maintained an independent French government since June 1940 did much to wipe out the shame of defeat and the armistice. The gradual disintegration of Vichy from 1942 onwards made the transition to the new form of government all the easier. De Gaulle was preoccupied with unity. He wanted all Frenchmen to continue united in the same patriotic determination as at the time of liberation. He formed a government which included a wide spectrum of political parties, including the Communists. He deliberately set out to make the purge less harsh (and he was assisted in this by the Communists), he disarmed the partisan groups and installed the regular authority of the state. He also emphasized the role of France in the world, all the more since the victorious allies were reluctant to accept France as one of the great powers. From 1940 de Gaulle had been greatly dependent upon gaining support in the French colonies and, appreciating the importance of the empire, he was anxious that the French position in Indo-China should be re-established.

A Constituent Assembly was elected in October 1945. Three-quarters of its members came from the Communists, the Socialists, or the new, largely Catholic, party which had been formed during the war, the MRP or Popular Republican Movement. During 1945 and 1946 they debated and voted a new constitution and new electoral laws, they nationalized key industries, introduced a comprehensive social security system and drew up a national plan for reconstruction and modernization. General de Gaulle was accepted as leader of the provisional government.

After the liberation of Paris, housewives pick up cabbage leaves outside the vegetable market.

The chubby, genial figure of
Maurice Thorez, Western
Europe's most influential post-
war Communist leader.

This has usually been described as a honeymoon period. In reality there was always a considerable amount of disagreement. General de Gaulle refused to apply the drastic economic and financial measures which his Finance Minister Pierre Mendès-France (b. 1907) had wanted to apply and he opted for René Pleven's (b. 1901) easier remedies, such as floating a loan. Mendès-France resigned in April 1945, and inflation was unchecked, causing a host of social and economic problems. De Gaulle was more concerned about the political evolution. When the old political structures began to re-appear, de Gaulle, who liked to think of himself as a man above parties, found himself increasingly ill at ease; he mistrusted the Communists because of their subservience to Soviet Russia; he was disappointed by the new constitution which was largely a replica of the Third Republic. There was to be no strong executive; governments were dependent upon the National Assembly; voting was by proportional representation so that a great many parties were likely to be returned. Therefore in January 1946 de Gaulle abruptly resigned. This marks the end of the period of provisional government and the beginning of the Fourth Republic.

The Fourth Republic seemed to have all the characteristics of the Third Republic. The governments were unstable, there was no coherent political majority, there was a constant shuffling and reshuffling of ministers. It even looked like the Third Republic when for a time in 1947 Léon Blum became Prime Minister, when Vincent Auriol (formerly his Finance Minister in the Popular Front government of 1936–37) was President of the Republic and

The Fourth Republic

Edouard Herriot, Prime Minister under the Third Republic, President of the National Assembly under the Fourth, also presided over the infant Council of Europe in 1949. Count and Countess Coudenhove-Kalergi, here seen talking to him, had dreamed of such a supranational union for twenty-five years.

Edouard Herriot President of the National Assembly. But if the Fourth Republic was like the Third, it was like the Third in its bad days, when there was a struggle to preserve a democratic way of life. As prices rose persistently, there were endless budgetary crises, wage disputes and strikes. The Communist party, which resigned from the coalition government in May 1947, remained a real and considerable force in French political life in spite of its isolation. In the autumn of 1947, there was a nation-wide strike. In October 1948 there was a vast mining strike. The trade-union movement was split among those who were Communist and the non-communists. France took on the appearance of a country torn by political and social divisions, with the largest political party, the Communists, apparently determined to destroy the system itself.

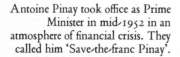

Antoine Pinay took office as Prime Minister in mid-1952 in an atmosphere of financial crisis. They called him 'Save-the-franc Pinay'.

This was intensified by the role played by de Gaulle. His resignation had not been a retirement. He maintained a close watch on affairs and continued to regard himself as the man who personified the unity of France. In April 1947 he founded an organization which he called the Rally of the French People (RPF) in order to emphasize that it was not a political party. But it behaved like a political party and it was highly successful in elections. Its first aim was to oppose the Communists. But fundamentally de Gaulle believed in a complete revision of the constitution. The Gaullists therefore, like the Communists, appeared as opponents of the régime itself. The Fourth Republic could only organize a Third Force, bringing together Socialists, Radicals and MRP in an uneasy coalition in which religious and social questions played a disruptive role.

Inflation and political instability were in themselves insoluble problems. But it was the colonial question which was to destroy the Fourth Republic. France was never an enthusiastic colonial power. In the late nineteenth century the acquisition of colonies had often been thought of as a deviation from the main issue, which was that of France's relations with Germany. However, the process of de-colonization was a painful experience. It began with Indo-China. *Colonial Retreat* There, as the French attempted to restore their pre-war position, they came into conflict with nationalists, the Viet Minh, led by Ho Chi Minh. By 1949 the French had set up a puppet Emperor, Bao Dai, whom they sponsored as the head of an independent Viet Nam state. But this was not successful. Year by year the French found themselves committed to an increasing expenditure of money and of men in a war which they did not seem able to win. In France itself, the Communists attacked the war and claimed that it was being fought in the interests of a small number of financiers and bankers. At one point the

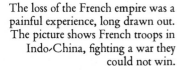
The loss of the French empire was a painful experience, long drawn out. The picture shows French troops in Indo-China, fighting a war they could not win.

General Vo Nguyen Giap (in black) led the Viet Minh in the successful siege of Dien Bien Phu. Defeat here in 1954 showed France that the war must be ended.

French army was reported to be losing an officer a day. When in May 1954 French troops suffered a major defeat at Dien Bien Phu, it became clear that this long and costly war could not be allowed to continue.

This situation was brought to an end by the most determined government of the Fourth Republic. In June 1954 Pierre Mendès-France shocked the Assembly into giving him a vote of confidence by promising to end the war in thirty days or to resign. In July 1954 the war was ended by the Geneva agreement, which established two independent states in Viet Nam (in addition to Cambodia and Laos).

The Mendès-France government attempted to retain the initiative which it had gained by bringing this war to an end. A dramatic visit to Tunis started the process whereby Tunisia would become a fully independent state and cease to be a French protectorate. In domestic affairs Mendès-France, who had been one of the youngest members of the Popular Front government, wanted to direct the economy towards greater efficiency and vitality. He appeared as a technocrat and a planner, trying to rationalize and modernize. For a time he was very popular and there seemed to be enthusiasm, especially among the young, for a government which was seeking to make a break with the past. But this popularity did not last. Indeed, Mendès-France was to become one of the least popular of French statesmen. He soon found that the central groups upon which he depended for his Parliamentary majority were deserting him. There was considerable opposition to him within his own party, the Radicals. He was reproached with having abandoned French territory, and the fact that he was Jewish encouraged some to suggest that he did not have the interests of France at heart. He was not an easy man to get on with and many deputies were glad to see him defeated in February 1955.

It was doubtless because he was conscious of this unpopularity that Mendès-France had reacted to the Algerian rebellion in November 1954, in a way that was typical of most politicians. He repeated the old claim that Algeria was French. With a European population of over 1 million, which sent deputies to sit in the Assembly in Paris, with prospects of great economic development

Pierre Mendès-France – the first French politician to realize that there was a young France.

and with communications becoming easier between France and Algeria every year, it seemed unthinkable that France would abandon this territory. The army, which included Moslem units, appeared certain to defeat the rebels, who did not seem to make much impact on the large and divided Moslem population as a whole (about 9 million). But experience was to show that the rebels could not be crushed. Successive French governments gave the army all the supplies that it required; they considered a variety of economic reforms within Algeria; they promised immediate victory. But the rebellion continued and became a revolution.

Within France itself the political confusion was considerable. In 1955 General de Gaulle dissociated himself from the RPF and devoted his time to writing his memoirs. The Communists remained strong but isolated. A new party, led by M. Pierre Poujade (b. 1920) emerged, which claimed to represent the small man in commercial and business enterprises; it was strong in the provinces, nationalistic and violent. Within the centre groups the Algerian war exacerbated the differences already existing among them; the elections of 1956 produced a government led by the Socialist Guy Mollet (b. 1905) with Mendès-France a member; within a few months Mendès-France had resigned; it was not long before the Socialists had withdrawn from office. No government seemed possible. It was as if the system was grinding to a halt. General de Gaulle, in his retirement at Colombey-les-deux-Eglises, was morose and pessimistic; Mendès-France spoke of France being in the situation of 1789.

Yet not everyone shared this attitude. The fact was that while France moved into a sort of political cul-de-sac, other things were happening which affected France profoundly. There was a boom which few people could have expected. From being a country where, as in the mid 1930's, the number of deaths exceeded the number of births, France became a country with a dynamic birth-rate. This tendency may have started about 1939–40; it may have been the result of governmental policies of family allowances; it might have been the effect of inflation, since it was inadvisable to save money and there was no incentive to practise birth-control; it may simply demonstrate a change in the whole attitude of French people to life in that, since 1940, the desire to have children has been stronger. At all events the population began to grow; it was typical of Mendès-France that he should have been the first politician to have realized that there was a young France.

The boom was also economic. The establishment, during the period of reconstruction, of a department for over-all economic planning which indicated

By the 1950's France was in a boom economy. The Rance tidal barrage (*above*) and the great petrochemical plant at Lacq (*below*) are two fruits of this time.

Above: Parly-Deux, on the outskirts of Paris, is a new concept in suburban living. *Below:* the Maison de Culture, in war-shattered Caen, is a project of André Malraux, Minister of Culture under de Gaulle.

Jean-Paul Sartre (*left*) and Albert Camus:
explorers of the absurdity of life.

the desirable direction for investment, began to yield results. By 1954 industrial production was 50 per cent higher than it had been prior to 1939. The steel industry, electrical power, the transport system, were all made more efficient. And in this shake-up of the French economy the idea that the once highly protected French market should be merged into a general European market was revolutionary. The idea that the future of France, both in terms of security and in terms of economic activity, was to be formed in specifically European organizations was attractive to many. It aroused great opposition but in 1958 France was a member both of the North Atlantic Treaty Organization and of the European Economic Community. With the exception of Algeria, the colonial problem moved nearer to solution as, from 1956 onwards, French African territories were granted autonomy. Intellectually, too, France was a great centre of attraction. The liberation had highlighted the writings of Jean-Paul Sartre (b. 1905) and Albert Camus (1913–60). They sought to explore the absurdity of life, to understand the extent to which man had freedom of choice. The great issues of the post-war world, the problems of progress and decay, of religious belief and Communism, of individual conviction and commitment, were treated in various art forms. It was as if France were pursuing its normal artistic role, and considering problems in a most articulate way.

Two giants from the past: Henri Matisse (*above*), seventy-five years old and crippled with arthritis, and Georges Braque, aged seventy-nine in 1960.

Any analysis of the situation in 1958 would have to look at the various centres of power which existed in France and in Algeria. There was firstly the normal, constitutional power of the French government, based upon the Assembly. But by April and May 1958, a prolonged ministerial crisis was demonstrating that this hardly existed. Then there was the power of the French army. This involved a great variety of opinion and attitudes, but after the defeat of 1940, the withdrawal from Indo-China in 1954, the experience of Suez in 1956 when Anglo-French forces had struck at Egypt but had been obliged to with-draw by international disapproval, and the experience of four years' war in Algeria, many of the army officers were discontented with their role. It seemed that to be an effective army they should extend their activity. They could not necessarily accept to play only a restricted and confined part in the affairs of the nation. Then there was the power of the settlers. By 1958 they were conscious of the threat to their privileged position in North Africa. They formed a great diversity of social existences and origins. But faced with this threat it was normal to emphasize the one thing that kept them all together: they were French. Around these centres of power French public opinion was largely indifferent and cynical. Amidst all the talk of financial crisis or of political violence, the public was accustoming itself to an early experience of affluence.

It was on 13 May 1958 that a number of students and political activists in Algiers, alarmed at the suggestion that the prolonged ministerial crisis would be ended by the appointment of a Prime Minister who would seek to make peace with the rebels, seized some government buildings. Self-consciously a Com-mittee of Public Safety was set up. This action did not have the expected effect. Premier Pierre Pflimlin (b. 1907) was given a vote of confidence in Paris. Thus there was a legal government in Paris and an illegal government in Algiers (and soon in other parts of Algeria). The army was uncertain of what should be done. Some officers were all for supporting the Algerian settlers and, if need be, seizing power in Paris. The French state appeared so weak that such an action seemed feasible. On the other hand, Communists, Socialists and those who can simply be called republicans showed signs of resisting such action. Many officers shrank from a blood-bath and sought to find some other way of saving the country from degradation.

It was in these circumstances that a great many turned to de Gaulle as the man whose prestige and patriotism seemed to offer the best prospects of avoiding civil war, and of finding some way out of the Algerian impasse. In this situation de Gaulle showed considerable skill and dexterity. He probably helped the situation to become worse, so that there was a general expectation that the parachutists might descend on Paris. At the same time he sought to reassure the normal centre of power, Parliament, that he did not intend to set up a dictatorship. On 27 May although the government of M. Pflimlin was still the legally constituted government, when de Gaulle announced that he was form- ing a government, there was no one who could take the responsibility of denying this. To have done so would have brought about a military operation and a left-wing riposte. On 1 June 1958 the Assembly voted full powers to de Gaulle.

If this was a revolution then it was very prolonged. A new constitution was to be devised, and it had to be approved by referendum in France and in the overseas territories; a general election had to be held; then a Presidential election had to take place in which the two chambers would combine with some 80,000 notables (mayors and municipal councillors) in forming an electoral college. The constitution was approved; a new Gaullist party, the Union of the New Republic (UNR) won a majority in the elections; de Gaulle was overwhelmingly elected President of the Republic and in January 1959 he installed himself at the Elysée Palace.

The Fifth Republic was in existence. But there was a great deal of speculation about its future. Many assumed that de Gaulle's tenure of office was bound to be short (he was sixty-nine when he became President). There was much speculation about what his policies would be and de Gaulle had deliberately cultivated ambiguity with regard to many vital questions, such as Algeria. Power was to be personalized in the one man who was always to remain some- what aloof and who sought to impose his own rhythm on the course of affairs. But essential to Gaullism were the circumstances in which the Fifth Republic had come into existence: the collapse of governmental power, the weakness of France in the world, the threat of civil war.

The period from 1958 to 1969 is that in which General de Gaulle was the dominant figure; it can conveniently be viewed in four sections. The first, beginning in 1958, was the institutional phase; the second, which necessarily began in 1958, too, was the settlement of the Algerian affair and it was con- cluded in 1962; the third, stretching from 1962 to 1966, can be described as the climax of Gaullism; a fourth period marks the decline of de Gaulle and is particularly apparent from 1967 to his resignation on 28 April 1969.

It is necessary to take the institutional phase first because de Gaulle himself undoubtedly regarded it as the most important. His enemies had likened his movement, in 1947, to Bonapartism or Boulangism because of his insistence upon a revision of the constitution. Thus in 1958, while the world wondered what he could do to settle the Algerian affair, de Gaulle's prime concern was to get the new constitution working. Algeria provided the opportunity whereby de Gaulle's constitutional ideas could be forced on a political community that would otherwise have rejected them.

The Fifth Republic   As it was, the constitution of the Fifth Republic was a very hybrid affair. It was based upon two apparently contradictory principles. The first was the belief in an essential unity within France. Nothing important could be decided without the consent of the French people. This was what de Gaulle meant when he called himself republican. The second was that there were basic divisions among the French people and that if these were given freedom then effective government would become impossible. Therefore there had to be strong, authoritarian government. Both these principles were incorporated in the constitution. The legislature continued to be the Chamber of Deputies (elected in single-member constituencies on a double-ballot system) and the Senate. A Prime Minister headed the government and although a number of procedural devices made it difficult, it was possible for the government to be overthrown by a hostile vote in Parliament. The President of the Republic was at first elected by a college of notables. He had considerable powers in normal conditions and in an emergency they could be increased still more. General de Gaulle showed how he wished to interpret his role as being the effective head of state. He took the decisions and announced them; there was no domain into which he could not venture; he could consult the people by referendum. In 1962, a constitutional change was brought about in the election of the President. Henceforward he was to be elected by universal suffrage.

Thus two systems existed side by side. There was the authoritarian government of the President, who saw himself as the leader of all the French people, in direct contact with them by election and by referendum. Then there was the Assembly, where the political parties continued to send representatives and to demonstrate their resilience. That there was no clash between them was largely due to the unique position of General de Gaulle. And whilst his strong personality and prestige contributed to this, much must also be explained in terms of the Algerian question.

It is not certain what General de Gaulle's ideas on Algeria were in 1958. He may well have had the hope that Algeria would fit in to the Community of African nations which was intended to be part of the 1958 constitution. By

Algérie française! In April 1961 the rebellious officers speak to the crowds from the balcony of the government building in Algiers. General Maurice Challe at the microphone; with him Generals Jouhaud (*left*) and Raoul Salan.

Armed troops face a watchful waiting crowd, as General de Gaulle visits Algeria.

The charismatic presence of de Gaulle, reaching out into the crowd, dissolved the tension. The Evian agreements paved the way to Algerian independence and an end to bitterness.

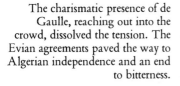

this each territory was to be autonomous, but would be associated in its foreign, strategic and economic policies with France. The President of the Republic was also to be President of the Community and his prestige in the world would be considerable. But de Gaulle was realistic and when, in 1960, he accepted that the African states wished to become fully independent, he probably accepted Algerian independence as well. He saw that France was being weakened in every way by the Algerian war. His problem was how to withdraw without risking conflict within France. He was helped in this by settler and military risings against him as well as by attempts to assassinate him. He also succeeded in allowing the situation to evolve with apparent gradualness. The result was that the Evian agreements of 1962 which ended the war and prepared the way for Algerian independence were approved by the over-whelming majority of the French. Out of the bitterness of the Algerian war a national unity had been created after all.

The third phase of Gaullism was marked by the display of Presidential power. A new Prime Minister, Georges Pompidou (b. 1911), was appointed who had never been a minister or a member of Parliament. General de Gaulle turned his attention towards economic affairs, and claimed that the economic expansion which was taking place was the result of stable government. It was certainly true that the settlers returning from Algeria were easily absorbed into a dynamic economy.

It was to foreign affairs that de Gaulle now gave most of his attention. He had always insisted that French defence should be in French hands and since he believed that the nation-state was the basis of all political life he had always been opposed to the establishment of supra-national European institutions. After 1962 he was able to act more freely. In 1963 he rejected the British application

The students' revolt of 1968. Police and students hurled stones at each other; the government appeared indecisive. 'Red Danny' Cohn-Bendit (turning left, in the foreground) was the most famous of the student leaders.

to join the Common Market; he began progressively to withdraw from NATO; by his policies towards Germany, Eastern Europe, the Soviet Union and China, he suggested that he was ready to challenge the United States of America. All this activity was demonstrated to the French public by the President's regular, though limited, television appearances. The French were made to believe that they were important in the world. It was widely assumed that the organization of Europe remained restricted to limited economic arrangements, because of French hostility to deeper integration.

But even at the height of this success de Gaulle was not completely secure. In the Presidential elections of 1965 he received only 43 per cent of the votes on the first ballot. That is to say that although he won on the second ballot when he was one of only two candidates, with 55 per cent of the votes cast, a majority of the population had clearly voted against him. This movement was to grow. The period of economic expansion came to an end and de Gaulle followed a deflationary policy, hoarding gold and seeking to challenge the dollar rather than to expand and modernize. This seemed to confirm the complaint of those who claimed that the working-class was not getting its share of prosperity and that Gaullism was really Conservatism. The elections of 1967 were unfavourable to the Gaullists and the extent of popular opposition was shown to be large. There was a reaction to the General's foreign policy and it was suggested that he could be too personal and temperamental in his actions. Above all, the General's age made it inevitable that there should be speculation about the future and that individuals and groups should be taking up their positions for the future.

Thus it was possible to talk of the break-up of Gaullism. Nevertheless, the events of May and June 1968 came as a surprise. A student revolt which put

De Gaulle condemned the student riots with military coarseness, calling them *chienlit*, 'shit-in-bed'. Student posters made suitably ribald response (*left*). Some believe that de Gaulle never recovered. Nearly a year later he resigned when defeated in a referendum. Amid the customary poster-war (*above*) a new president was elected – the General's former adviser and friend, Georges Pompidou.

some of the streets and buildings of Paris into their hands was followed by a vast movement of strikes. The government appeared powerless and de Gaulle considered resignation. But on 30 May 1968 he announced that he would not resign and that the Chamber was dissolved. In the ensuing elections the threat of anarchy if de Gaulle disappeared from the scene seemed real enough for a considerable Gaullist majority to be returned. The régime even appeared to emerge strengthened from the crisis and de Gaulle replaced Pompidou by Couve de Murville (b. 1907) who had been a loyal Foreign Minister since 1958.

Les Evénements

However, in some respects Gaullism was compromised. De Gaulle had been severely shaken; he had won the elections by attacking the Communists and Gaullism could no longer claim to represent the whole of France, but only a portion of France; many Gaullists wondered if de Gaulle were not a liability, especially since in Pompidou they saw his obvious successor. When de Gaulle, claiming that the events of 1968 had demonstrated the need for a profound modification of the system of centralization, asked that such a reform should be approved by referendum, he found a united opposition against him. On 27 April 1969 a majority of the French population voted against the referendum and de Gaulle immediately resigned.

Like other French rulers de Gaulle left power apparently unregretted. The institutions continued to function and M. Pompidou was duly elected to the

173

Still France remained stubbornly disunited: farmers blocking the roads in protest at low prices for their produce were not the only group to defend their interests with violence.

Presidency. A Prime Minister, Jacques Chaban-Delmas (b. 1915), was chosen from among the Gaullist faithful. Gaullist foreign policies were made to appear less intransigent rather than substantially modified. The government avoided any profound reforms and sought to preserve the unity of the Gaullist party.

Outside this party all the signs were of division. There was no collaboration among Communists or Socialists. The students remained in over-crowded universities and, facing employment difficulties, remained restive. Small groups, especially shopkeepers and the farmers who remained on the land after so many had left, sought to defend their interests, if necessary by violent means. Old political organizations, like the Radical party, began new offensives in order to assert their position. New and sometimes shadowy groups of the left and right appeared. Intellectuals were increasingly cut off from the remainder of society. The government was preoccupied by law and order. Technicians sought to make the French economy more efficient. Others were concerned that the social contrasts among the French people were becoming more strident. Personalities such as Jean-Jacques Servan-Schreiber (b. 1924) called for new ideas and methods. But in spite of being a member of the European Economic Community and in spite of the extension of the consumer society, the structures and the ideals of the French nation were slow to change.

Chapter Eight

CONCLUSIONS

Historians of France have often spoken about the ghosts of French history. They have suggested that as one epoch of French history succeeds another, the characteristics of earlier ages are repeated. Sometimes this is seen in a general way, with successive periods of strong authority, such as the Roman Empire, Charlemagne, Louis XIV, Bonaparte, Napoleon III, Pétain and de Gaulle, being placed among periods of division and anarchy. Sometimes it is seen more precisely, and it is said that the period of the bourgeois revolution from 1789 to 1792 was re-enacted from 1815 to 1848; then the popular and socialist phase of the Revolution recurred in 1848; the concluding phases of the Revolution, the Directory, the Consulate and the Empire saw their equivalents in the Presidency of Louis-Napoleon and in the Second Empire. But however this

Symbol of the greatness of France – the Palace of Versailles.

is put, the result is the same. The impression is gained that one can have faith in the destiny of France. Conquest, invasion, civil war, have never lasted. There has always been resistance and recovery.

Most writers on France have also thrown emphasis on diversity. In historical, geographical and ideological terms the French have always been extremely varied. Sometimes the idea has been put forward that there are two Frances: revolutionary and counter-revolutionary, clerical and anti-clerical, Dreyfusard and anti-Dreyfusard, left and right. Often it has been claimed that there are a great many Frances, that in fact France is the country where the most divergent opinions can be held and where they can all be considered justified. France therefore is the country of division, strife and disagreement. It is because of this that French history is unusually dramatic; it is on account of this that the Frenchman is given to logic and the spirit of party rather than to common sense and compromise. And the impression is gained that within all this discord there must be an essential unity of France and the French. Perhaps the diversity creates its own harmony as in a medieval feud. Perhaps there is a real unity there which can respond to a Capetian, a Bourbon, a Bonaparte or a de Gaulle.

Then there are the paradoxes of French history. The French state has for long been strong and centralized, with extensive fiscal and military rights; yet it has always been fragile and it has invariably been contested. The course of French history has been marked by change and revolution; yet political change has often been accepted as a substitute for more profound social development. Great men have appeared who have made an indelible mark upon the French past; yet they have rarely been great reformers, and instead of extensively modifying the structure of society, they have usually been content to introduce a little efficiency into the existing system. Frenchmen, it is said, have wished to be barefoot, and to follow Napoleon to the ends of the earth; at the same time they have wished for their comforts, for an early bed and a good bed. Collectively, the French have pursued equality; individually, the Frenchman has pursued privilege. It is significant that there is a certain ambiguity both about many of the great individuals of French history and about many institutions.

Historians, therefore, have been tempted to exploit these complexities. As research progresses, more and more detail is amassed which demonstrates that French history is even more varied than has been thought; generalizations and simplifications are increasingly made to appear suspect and irrelevant. Yet in France the national consciousness is a historical consciousness. This is most obvious in modern times when certain episodes have become occasions for a

Great men have made an indelible mark – 'Père-la-victoire': the ▶
Clemenceau statue in the Champs Elysées.

new kind of consciousness to define itself. If men such as Napoleon and de Gaulle have made such an impression on France, this is more a commentary on France than upon them. The year 1789 and the revolutions of the nineteenth century; the Dreyfus affair; the two world wars of the twentieth century; the revolutions of 1958 and 1968. For the French this history is all contemporary history. It is as if France needs history. A Frenchman has been defined as someone who knows his history.

When we study France we study a country which has always been conscious of playing a role on the world stage and a people who are aware of the adventures of French history. It is because of this that a Frenchman said that Europe only learns something properly once the French have explained it, and a Frenchwoman said that France thinks the thoughts that the world has need of.

A history-conscious cartoonist sums up, 'with apologies to David' (*see p. 115*).

List of Illustrations

179

26 Baptism of Clovis. Detail from a 9th century diptych of carved ivory showing the Life of St Rémy. *Musée de Picardie, Amiens.*

27 The Gold Reliquary of St Maurice d'Agaune, decorated with pearls, garnets and coloured pastes, 8th century. *Abbaye de St Maurice, France.*

28 The Emperor Charlemagne enthroned, *c.* 1200. Stained glass from Strasbourg Cathedral. Musée de l'Oeuvre, Notre Dame. *Photo Musées de la Ville de Strasbourg.*

29 Charlemagne's Empire.

30 Ivory cover of the prayer book of Charles the Bald, *c.* 870. *Schweizerisches Landesmuseum, Zurich.*

33 Soldiers, councillors, churchmen, peasants, craftsmen and merchants. From a 14th century MS. 11201–2, fol. 2632. *Bibliothèque Royale, Brussels.*

34 Ploughing, from MS, Cotton Aug. V, fol. 161v. *By courtesy of the Trustees of the British Museum.*

Detail of a covered wagon and barges carrying barrels of wine, from a miniature of the *Life of St Denis.* MS. Fr 2091, fol. 125. *Bibliothèque Nationale, Paris.*

35 Street with shops from *Gouvernement des Princes,* by Frère Gilles. From a 15th century MS. 5062, fol. 149. Arsenal Library, Paris. *Photo Giraudon.*

The bishop of Paris blessing the Lendit fair. From the *Grandes Chroniques de France,* 14th century MS. Lat. 962–264. *Bibliothèque Nationale, Paris.*

36 Henry I granting a charter to a monastery. From a chronicle of the abbey of St Martin des Champs, 1067. Add. MS. 11662. *By courtesy of the Trustees of the British Museum, London.*

Father arranging for his son to be educated by monks. From a 13th century MS. w 133, fol. 87. *Walters Art Gallery, Baltimore.*

37 Monks at a service in the choir. MS. Cotton Dom. A. XVII, fol. 122v, early 14th century. *By courtesy of the Trustees of the British Museum, London.*

Monk (cellarer) tippling. From a 13th century health manual of Aldebrandius of Siena, MS. SI 2435, fol. 44v. *By courtesy of the Trustees of the British Museum, London.*

Capital from the third abbey church of Cluny, showing the first tone of the Gregorian chant, 1088–95. *Musée Ochier, Cluny.*

38 Tympanum of the abbey church of St Pierre, Moissac, *c.* 1100. *Photo Giraudon.*

Interior of the abbey church of La Madeleine, Vezelay, looking east, showing the 12th century nave. *Photo Archives Photographiques.*

Isaiah, from the doorway of Souillac, Quercy, *c.* 1130–40. *Photo Jean Roubier.*

39 Benedictine abbey of Jumièges dedicated to Notre Dame. Ruins of the transept, nave and central tower. *Photo Archives Photographiques.*

View of the cloister of Mont-Saint-Michel, completed 1228. *Photo Archives Photographiques.*

40 Detail of the Bayeux Tapestry, showing William of Normandy riding to join the invasion fleet, mid 11th century. Ancien Evêché, Bayeux. *Photo Giraudon.*

41 Detail of a stained glass window, showing Abbot Suger. The glass, dating from the mid 12th century, is set in a 13th century window showing scenes from the life of the Virgin. *Photo Jean Roubier.*

42 Wooden statue of Saint Louis (Louis IX). Musée Cluny, Paris. *Photo Giraudon/Mansell.*

43 The Château de Fougères. *Photo Yvon.*

45 Froissart presenting his book to the comte de Foix. Scene from the *Froissart Chronicles,* late 15th century MS. Royal 14 D.V., fol. 8. *By courtesy of the Trustees of the British Museum, London.*

47 The arrival of St Denis in Paris. Illumination from the *Légende de St Denis,* 14th century MS. Fonds Fr. 2090–92. *Bibliothèque Nationale, Paris.*

48 Student life from the statute of the College of Ave Maria, Paris, dating from the 14th century *Ordonnances de l'Hôtel du Roy.* Archives Nationales, Paris. *Photo Giraudon.*

49 Amiens cathedral. *Photo Bulloz.*

Miniature from the *Roman de la Rose.* From a 15th-century MS. Harley 4431. *By courtesy of the Trustees of the British Museum, London.*

Sculptured figures from Chartres cathedral. Detail of the south door showing Music and Grammar with Pythagoras and Donatus, mid 12th century. *Photo Bildarchiv Foto Marburg.*

50 The Black Death at Tournai, 1349. From Gilles le Muisit's *Annales*, 1352 (MS. 13076-77, fol. 24v). Bibliothèque Royale de Belgique, Brussels. *Photo Giraudon.*

51 The Coronation of Charles VI, from late 14th-century *Chroniques de Saint Denis* (MS. Royal 20, c. VII, fol. 216). *By courtesy of the Trustees of the British Museum, London.*

The king of England doing homage to the king of France. From the late 14th-century *Chroniques de Saint Denis* (MS. Royal 20, c. VII, fol. 720). *By courtesy of the Trustees of the British Museum, London.*

52 Joan of Arc at the stake. From the *Vigils of Charles VII*, 1484 (MS. fr. 5054, fol. 71). Bibliothèque Nationale, Paris. *Photo Bulloz.*

53 Carving of a ship from the lintel of the house of Jacques Cœur, Bourges. *Photo Archives Photographiques.*

54 Louis XI. Burgundian School. *Photo Mansell Collection.*

56 Hospices de Beaune, Côte d'Or, founded by Nicholas Rolin 1443-49. *Photo Camera Press Ltd.*

57 Detail from the *Très Riches Heures du Duc de Berry*, showing the Ile de la Cité. Dating from June 1413-16, MS. 65, fol. 6v. Musée Condé, Chantilly. *Photo Giraudon.*

Detail of the Vintage Tapestry (right side). Dating from the latter part of the 15th century. Musée Cluny, Paris. *Photo Giraudon.*

Detail of Tournai tapestry showing hunting and hawking, c. 1440. Formerly in the collection of the duke of Devonshire. *Victoria and Albert Museum, London. Crown copyright.*

58 Detail of doorway, Saint-Maclou, Rouen. *Photo French Government Tourist Office.*

59 French astrolabe, late 15th century. *The Science Museum, London.*

61 Medallion of Louis XII, designed by Nicholas Leclerc and Jean de Saint-Priest, cast by Jean and Colin Lepère. *Bibliothèque Nationale, Paris.*

62 Equestrian portrait of Francis I. School of Clouet. *Musée Condé, Chantilly.*

63 Marguerite d'Angoulême presenting her MS. to the Duchesse d'Etampes, 16th century. MS. 522/1878. Musée Condé, Chantilly. *Photo Giraudon.*

64 Château de Blois. Staircase tower, Francis I wing. *Photo Helga Schmidt-Glassner.*

Château de Chambord. Porte Royale side. *Photo Bildarchiv Foto Marburg.*

65 Fontainebleau. Galerie Francis I. *Photo Giraudon.*

66 Map of Paris, by Truschet and Hoyau, showing the university quarter, 1550-52. *Bibliothèque de la Ville, Basle.*

67 Gouache copy of the 'Tapestry Plan', showing Paris c. 1540. *Photo Giraudon.*

68 Portrait of Calvin lecturing, sketched in 1564 by a student, Jacques Bourgoing de Nevers, in his copy of Robert Gaguin's *Compendium super Francorum Gestis*, 1511. *Bibliothèque Publique et Universitaire, Geneva.*

69 Catherine de' Medici as a widow. Drawing by François Clouet, c. 1560. *Bibliothèque Nationale, Paris.*

70 Henry III. Drawing by François Clouet, 1571. *Bibliothèque Nationale, Paris.*

Ball given at the court of Henry III in honour of the marriage of the Duc de Joyeuse. French School, late 16th century. Louvre, Paris. *Photo Giraudon.*

71 Henry IV. French School, late 16th century. Musée de Peinture, Grenoble. *Photo Giraudon.*

72 France at the end of the 16th century.

Portrait of Madame de Pompadour, by François Boucher, 1758. *Victoria and Albert Museum, London. Crown copyright.*

99 *Building a Road*, by Joseph Vernet, 1774. Louvre, Paris. *Photo Royal Academy of Arts, London*

100 *Return from the Christening*, by Louis le Nain. Louvre, Paris. *Photo Giraudon.*

The Swing, by Honoré Fragonard, 1767. *Wallace Collection, London.*

101 Portrait of Rousseau, by Allan Ramsay, 1766. *By courtesy of the National Gallery of Scotland, Edinburgh.*

Le Repas des philosophes, showing Diderot, Condorcet and d'Alembert. Engraving by Jean Huber. British Museum, London. *Photo John R. Freeman.*

102 Drawing of Louis XVI, by Ducreux. Musée Carnavalet, Paris. *Photo Bulloz.*

104 The first Channel crossing by balloon, 1785, by Blanchard and Jeffries. *Photo Mansell Collection.*

105 *Le Rappel de Monsieur Necker.* Engraving *c.* 1788. *Bibliothèque Nationale, Paris.*

106 *Le Reveil du Tiers Etat*; 'The Awakening of the Third Estate'. Coloured engraving, 1789. Bibliothèque Nationale, Paris. *Photo Françoise Foliot.*

107 Declaration of the Rights of Man, 26 August 1789. Bibliothèque Nationale, Paris. *Photo Giraudon.*

108 March of the Women to Versailles, 5 October 1789. Bibliothèque Nationale, Paris. *Photo Giraudon.*

109 'The three orders hammering out the new constitution'. Popular print, *c.* 1791. British Museum, London. *Photo John R. Freeman.*

Marie-Antoinette with her children, by Madame Vigée-Lebrun. Musée de Versailles. *Photo Giraudon.*

110 'The money of the Republic'. Popular print, *c.* 1792. British Museum, London. *Photo John R. Freeman.*

111 A revolutionary committee. Engraving from the *Collection des tableaux historiques de la Révolution Française*, 1804.

Attack on the Tuileries, 10 August 1792. Painting by Jacques Bertaux. Musée de Versailles. *Photo Giraudon.*

112 The execution of Louis XVI, 21 January 1793. Engraving by Helman. *Photo Mansell Collection.*

Portrait of Robespierre, by an unknown artist. From a facsimile. British Museum, London. *Photo John R. Freeman.*

113 The triumphal entry of monuments into Paris, 6 February 1798. Engraving by Pierre Gabriel Berthault from a drawing by Girardet. *By courtesy of the Trustees of the British Museum, London.*

114 Napoleon as First Consul visiting the textile factory of the Severin brothers at Rouen in 1802. Painting by Isabey. Musée de Versailles. *Photo Musées Nationaux.*

115 Portrait of Napoleon in coronation robes, by Ingres, 1806. Musée de l'Armée, Paris. *Photo Giraudon.*

Napoleon preparing to crown himself. A sketch by Jacques-Louis David. In the final version, 1805–7, Napoleon extends the crown towards Josephine. Louvre, Paris. *Photo Françoise Foliot.*

116 Bivouac of Napoleon on the eve of Austerlitz. Painting by Lejeune, 1803. Musée de Versailles. *Photo Mansell-Bulloz.*

117 Drawing of Louis XVII. Musée Carnavalet, Paris. *Photo Bulloz.*

Le grand casse-noisette du 25 juillet. Caricature of Charles X. *Photo Mansell Collection.*

118 Photograph of Louis-Philippe, taken in June 1845. *Photo Mansell Collection.*

Haussmann presenting his plans to the Emperor Napoleon III. Bibliothèque Historique de la Ville de Paris. *Photo Bulloz.*

119 Portrait of Guizot, by Say. Author's Collection. *Photo Eileen Tweedy.*

120 Chateaubriand, by Girodet. Musée de Versailles. *Photo Bulloz.*

121 'Le ventre législatif'. Caricature by Daumier. Lithograph from *L'Association Mensuelle*, February 1834. *Photo Giraudon.*

122 Balzac, Lemaître and Gautier. Painting by Gautier. Private Collection. *Photo Bulloz.*

123 The Quai du Louvre, Paris. Painting by Monet, 1866–67. *Gemeentemuseum, The Hague.*

125 Le Mur des Fédérés: the execution of 28 May 1871. Drawing by H. A. Darjou, Musée Carnavalet, Paris. *Photo Giraudon.*

126 Adolphe Thiers (1797–1877). *The Radio Times Hulton Picture Library.*

A Parisian street during the Commune, 1871. *Photo Mansell Collection.*

127 The Rue des Abbesses. Painting by Maurice Utrillo, *c.* 1913. *Private Collection, New York.*

128 Caricature of Marshal MacMahon. *Photo Sirot.*

129 Adolphe Thiers receiving an ovation in the Chamber of Deputies, 16 June 1877. Painting by B. Ulmann. Musée de Versailles. *Photo Giraudon.*

132 General Boulanger. *Photo Sirot.*

Cartoon of Boulangism, 1887. *Photo Mansell Collection.*

133 Captain Dreyfus after the re-trial at Rennes, 1899. *Photo Radio Times Hulton Picture Library.*

134 A detail from a contemporary cartoon called 'Histoire d'un Innocent'. Detail shows France hovering over the rehabilitated Dreyfus. *Photo Sirot.*

135 Medal struck to commemorate the building of the Eiffel Tower, 1889. *Photo Mansell Collection.*

136 Marcel Proust (1871–1922). *Photo Mansell Collection.*

Claude Debussy (1862–1918). *Photo Radio Times Hulton Picture Library.*

Verlaine and Rimbaud. Detail from the painting *Un coin de table* by Fantin Latour. Louvre, Paris. *Photo Giraudon.*

André Gide (1869–1951), by J.-E. Blanche, 1912. Musée des Beaux Arts, Rouen. *Photo Ellebé.*

137 General Marchand and his staff at Fashoda. *Photo Radio Times Hulton Picture Library.*

English caricature of the Fashoda incident, 18 October 1898. *Photo Radio Times Hulton Picture Library.*

138 French detachment moving up to support the Belgians along the Yser canal, 1914. *Photo Mansell Collection.*

A French poster selling victory bonds. *Photo Camera Press.*

139 French wounded in a farm after the Champagne offensive, October 1915. *Photo Radio Times Hulton Picture Library.*

140 General Foch signing Armistice, 1918. *Gernsheim Collection, University of Texas.*

141 Clemenceau with General Pinney (33rd division), Cassel, 21 April 1918. *Photo Imperial War Museum.*

142 Signing of the Versailles Peace Treaty, 1919. *Photo Roger-Viollet.*

Messieurs Maginot, Poincaré, Lefèvre and Marshal Pétain at Verdun station in 1920. *Photo Sirot.*

143 Herriot and Beneš at Geneva. *Photo Sirot.*

144 Briand leaving the British Foreign Office in 1925. *Photo Radio Times Hulton Picture Library.*

145 Ruins of a barricade in the Boulevard Sébastopol, after the French police had driven off demonstrators, during the Stavisky Riots, Paris 1934. *Photo Radio Times Hulton Picture Library.*

Léon Blum leaving his house for the Chamber of Deputies on the eve of becoming Prime Minister in 1936. *Photo Sirot.*

147 Changing guard in the Maginot Line, 1940. *Photo Associated Press.*

British and French prisoners at Dunkirk, 1940. *Photo Imperial War Museum.*

Index

Page numbers in italics refer to illustration captions